MENTORING
and MODELING

Developing the next generation

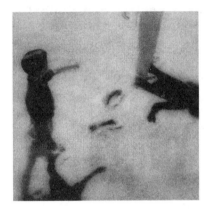

Dr. John Goetsch
Dr. Mark Rasmussen

Published by:

Revival Books and
West Coast Baptist College
A ministry of Lancaster Baptist Church
4020 E. Lancaster Blvd.
Lancaster, CA 93535
661-946-2274
www.westcoastbaptist.edu
E-mail: wcbaptist@aol.com

Cover Design and Layout:
Craig Parker

ISBN 0-9726506-1-X

Printed in the United States of America.

Contents

Dedication

This book is dedicated to our wives:
Diane Goetsch and Suza Rasmussen

And our children:
John, Melinda, Brock, and Eric Goetsch
Amy, Alisa, and Mark Rasmussen

Who have been patient with us as husbands
and dads while we've tried to learn ourselves
the principles of that which we preach, teach, and write.

Introduction

There is an old Chinese Proverb that says:
>If you are planting for a year, plant grain.
>If you are planting for a decade, plant trees.
>If you are planting for a century, plant people.

As Christians, we are planting for eternity! The ministry today screams at us to preach effective sermons, teach dynamic lessons, run great youth activities, write a best-selling book, or lead a life-changing seminar. Church leaders are caught in the never-ending maze of organization and administration, while parents are working day and night to provide the "best that money can buy" for their children. And although the youth of today are hearing great sermons, participating in fabulous and expensive activities, attending schools with outstanding curriculum, and enjoying the materialism of our age, they are sadly growing up without a mentor. Ron Lee Davis states: "For all the thousands who are eager to share their knowledge and skills with others, there are just a handful who are willing to share their LIVES, who are willing to be transparent, vulnerable, and open about their successes and their failures, their joys and their pain, their faith and their doubts."[1]

The term "mentor" does not appear in the Scriptures. In fact, it comes from the name of a character in Homer's Odyssey. In this ancient Greek tale, King Odysseus of Ithaca entrusted his only son, Telemachus, to the care and training of his wise friend, Mentor, while he himself went off to war. In the character of Homer's Mentor, we find the ingredients of wisdom, caring, and commitment to train this young man for his master.

This idea is not strange to the business world, where apprenticeships are often served and the skills and knowledge of the experienced are transmitted to the inexperienced. It would be rare indeed to find a success in the political, business, athletic, or social world that did not train under someone else. Yet, as parents, preachers, and teachers, we tend to guard our privacy, not wanting those watching to know us too well. We seem content to impress from a distance, which is easily done, but hesitate to impact up close, which is what our Lord exemplified for us in His life and ministry.

Jesus transformed the world because He poured His life into the Twelve. Though He preached to the masses, He invested Himself in a few, knowing that those few would invest themselves in still others, and thus transform the world. If we want to transform our families, our churches, our businesses, our communities, and ultimately our world, then we must discover what it means to pour our lives into individuals. We must learn to spend more time with the few. We must learn to live for the next generation. We must become mentors.[2]

---

[1] Ron Lee Davis, _Mentoring: The Strategy of the Master,_ Nashville, TN, Thomas Nelson, 1991, p. 23.
[2] Ibid, p. 21.

This principle is as old as the Bible itself. Proverbs 27:17 states: "Iron sharpeneth iron; so a man sharpeneth the countenance of his friend." Over and over again on the pages of Scripture we see this practice in action. Moses mentored Joshua. Naomi mentored her daughter-in-law, Ruth. Ezra mentored Nehemiah. Elijah mentored Elisha. Elisabeth mentored her cousin Mary. Barnabas mentored Paul and John Mark. Paul mentored Timothy and also Priscilla and Aquila, who in turn mentored Apollos.

In Matthew 28:19-20, Jesus said: "Go ye therefore, and teach all nations, baptizing them in the name of the Father, and of the Son, and of the Holy Ghost: Teaching them to observe all things whatsoever I have commanded you: and, lo, I am with you alway, even unto the end of the world." The mandate here cannot be misunderstood: Evangelize – Baptize – Disciple! We must win people to Christ by telling them the Good News of the Gospel, baptize these converts, and then begin the life-long process of teaching. And none of us are exempt from carrying out any part of this commission. We do not get to choose whether or not we want to be involved in soul winning – we are commanded to share the Gospel. Likewise, we cannot excuse ourselves from the teaching process. Whether we are a parent, pastor, youth leader, Sunday School teacher, Christian school teacher, or just a friend, we have a command from God to teach.

John Milton Gregory says, "True teaching, then, is not that which gives knowledge, but that which stimulates pupils to gain it. One might say that he teaches best who teaches least; or that he teaches best whose pupils learn most without being taught directly. Two meanings of the word teaching are involved, one, simply telling, the other creating the conditions of real learning."[3] Dennis H. Dirks states: "God has chosen teachers to be instruments of promoting change. The root meaning of the word "educate" is to draw out rather than to fill with facts. It may be compared with the role of a midwife or obstetrician. The birth attendant does not merely tell the mother all she needs to know about the birth process. The attendant helps make the birth possible."[4]

When Jesus taught the disciples about being a servant, He not only gave them a verbal lesson, He also washed their feet. Not only did He teach them what to pray, He took them to the garden and prayed with them. He taught them with more than words – He immersed them in the very experiences of His life.

Somehow today, we have reduced our ministry down to an eight-hour-a-day job at the Christian school, or a youth activity on Saturday night, or a Sunday school lesson on Sunday morning. We have neatly packaged our ministry into sermons, lessons, assignments, and sessions. We are irritated when our schedule is interrupted by people with problems, questions, and needs. We have convinced ourselves that if people have our e-mail address, the number to our answering machine, and the password into our voice-message box, we are available. We have become masters at managing, but miserable at mentoring.

The Apostle Paul, in I Timothy 4:16, admonishes young Timothy: "Take heed unto thyself and unto the doctrine; continue in them: for in doing this thou shalt both save thyself, and them that hear thee." There is no question that proper doctrine is

---

[3] John Milton Gregory, _The Seven Laws of Teaching_, Grand Rapids, MI, Baker Book, Revised Edition – 1954 from the 1917 edition as published by the Pilgrim Press, p. 77.

[4] Dennis H. Dirks, _Christian Education: Foundations for the Future_, Chicago, IL, Moody Press, 1991, p. 138.

important and that we must equip ourselves to teach the truths of God's Word. But it is interesting that Paul first tells Timothy to take heed unto himself! The Christian life is not just about doctrine and dogma – it's about character – Christ-like character. The goal of the Christian life according to Romans 8:29 is ". . . to be conformed to the image of his Son." Paul knew that this kind of teaching was "better caught than taught!" That's why when Jesus called the Twelve, He didn't say, "Listen to me." He said, "Follow me."

It is time for a paradigm shift in our thinking about what ministry is all about. It's more than neatly designed lesson plans, exegetically correct sermons, and smooth-running activities – it's about PEOPLE! People that God has entrusted to us to mentor.

The following story illustrates well the challenge and joy of this momentous task:

Teddy Stallard certainly qualified as "one of the least." He was disinterested in school, musty, had wrinkled clothes, his hair never combed. He was one of those kids in school with a deadpan face, expressionless – sort of a glassy, unfocused stare. When Miss Thompson spoke to Teddy, he always answered in monosyllables. Unattractive, unmotivated, and distant, he was just plain hard to like. Even though his teacher said she loved all in her class the same, down inside she wasn't being completely truthful.

Whenever she marked Teddy's papers, she got a certain perverse pleasure out of putting X's next to the wrong answers, and when she put the F's at the top of his papers, she always did it with a flair. She should have known better; she had seen Teddy's records, and she knew more about him than she wanted to admit. The records read:

1st Grade:	*Teddy shows promise with his work and attitude, but poor home situation.*
2nd Grade:	*Teddy could do better. Mother is seriously ill. He receives little help at home.*
3rd Grade:	*Teddy is a good boy but too serious. He is a slow learner. His mother died this year.*
4th Grade:	*Teddy is very slow, but well behaved. His father shows no interest.*

Christmas came, and the boys and girls in Miss Thompson's class brought her Christmas presents. They piled their presents on her desk and crowded around to watch her open them. Among the presents was one from Teddy Stallard. She was surprised that he had brought her a gift. Teddy's gift was wrapped in brown paper and was held together with Scotch tape. On the paper were written the simple words, "For Miss Thompson from Teddy." When she opened Teddy's present, out fell a gaudy rhinestone bracelet with half the stones missing and a bottle of cheap perfume.

The other boys and girls began to giggle and smirk over Teddy's gift, but Miss Thompson at least had enough sense to silence them by immediately putting on the bracelet and putting some of the perfume on her wrist. Holding her wrist for the other children to smell, she said, "Doesn't it smell lovely?" And the other children, taking their cues from the teacher, readily agreed with "oohs" and "aahs."

At the end of the day, when school was over and the other children had left, Teddy lingered behind. He slowly came over to her desk and said softly, "Miss Thompson . . . Miss Thompson, you smell just like my mother . . . and her bracelet looks real pretty on you, too. I'm glad you like my presents."

When Teddy left, Miss Thompson got down on her knees and asked God to forgive her.

The next day when the children came to school, a new teacher welcomed them. Miss Thompson had become a different person. She was no longer just a teacher; she had become an agent of God. She was now a person committed to loving her children and doing things for them that would live on after her. She helped all the children, but especially the slow ones, and especially Teddy Stallard. By the end of that school year, Teddy showed dramatic improvement. He had caught up with most of the students and was even ahead of some.

She didn't hear from Teddy for a long time. Then one day, she received a note that read:

Dear Miss Thompson,

I wanted you to be the first to know. I will be graduating second in my class.

Love,

Teddy Stallard

Four years later, another note came:

Dear Miss Thompson,

They just told me I will be graduating first in my class. I wanted you to be the first to know. The university has not been easy, but I liked it.

Love,

Teddy Stallard

And four years later:

Dear Miss Thompson,

As of today, I am Theodore Stallard, MD. How about that? I wanted you to be the first to know. I am getting married next month, the 27th to be exact. I want you to come and sit where my mother would sit if she were alive. You are the only family I have now; Dad died last year.
Love,
Teddy Stallard

Miss Thompson went to that wedding and sat where Teddy's mother would have sat. She deserved to sit there; she had done something for Teddy that he could never forget.[5]

If I had my life to live over again, I would live it to change the lives of people, because you have not changed anything until you've changed the lives of people. - Missionary Warren Webster

---

[5] Anthony Campolo, _Who Switched the Price Tags?_, Waco, TX, Word Books, 1986, pp. 69-72.

Part I

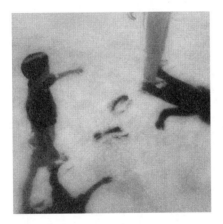

By Dr. John Goetsch

---◇---

CHAPTER ONE

Maturity or Mediocrity

"Therefore to him that knoweth to do good, and doeth it not, to him it is sin." James 4:17

After an eighteen-month study, the National Commission on Excellence in Education issued a report in April of 1983 entitled "A Nation at Risk." The report stated: "The educational foundations of our society are presently being eroded by a rising tide of mediocrity that threatens our very future as a nation and as a people." The Presidential Commission added these chilling words: "If an unfriendly foreign power had attempted to impose on America the mediocre educational performance that exists today, we might well have viewed it as an act of war. As it stands, we have allowed this to happen to ourselves."[1]

Our God is a God of excellence. Psalms 8:9 says: "O Lord our Lord, how excellent is thy name in all the earth!" Philippians 1:10 makes it clear that we are ". . . to approve things that are

---

[1] John A. Stormer, *None Dare Call It Education*, Florissant, MO, Liberty Bell Press, 1998, p. 8.

excellent." Our flesh, however, is always looking for a shortcut, an easier way, or something with a little less sacrifice. And soon...

Excellence gets reduced to Acceptable,

And then, Acceptable gets reduced to Adequate,

And then, Adequate becomes Mediocre,

And Mediocrity is Sin!

Mentoring the next generation must have as its goal the excellency of Christian maturity. Can there be any doubt in Paul's desire for his life from his words in Philippians 3:8-10? "Yea doubtless, and I count all things but loss for the excellency of the knowledge of Christ Jesus my Lord: for whom I have suffered the loss of all things, and do count them but dung, that I may win Christ, And be found in him, not having mine own righteousness, which is of the law, but that which is through the faith of Christ, the righteousness which is of God by faith: That I may know him, and the power of his resurrection, and the fellowship of his sufferings, being made conformable unto his death."

Perry G. Downs states: "The organizing principle of the educational ministry of the church should be the spiritual growth of her people. Her central task is to produce people who are spiritually mature."[2] God's goal for His people is conformity to the image of His Son (Romans 8:29). If our goal as parents, pastors, and teachers is anything less than that, the potential of our children will be destroyed by our sinful mediocrity. John Gardner sums it up quite well when he says: "Our society cannot achieve greatness unless individuals at many levels of ability accept the need for high standards of performance and strive to achieve those

---

[2] Perry G. Downs, *Teaching for Spiritual Growth*, Grand Rapids, MI, Zondervan, 1994, pp. 197-198.

standards within the limits possible for them. . . . We cannot have islands of excellence in a sea of sloven indifference. . . ."[3]

He later adds: "We accept all kinds of shoddy education that is no more than going through the motions. We pretend that so many courses, so many credits, so many hours in the classroom, so many books add up to an education. . . . We seem immensely satisfied with the outer husk of the enterprise – the number of dollars spent, the size of the laboratories, the number of people involved, the fine projects outlined, the number of publications. Why do we grasp so desperately at externals? Partly because. . . it is easier to organize the external aspects of things. The mercurial spirit of great teaching and great scholarship cannot be organized, rationalized, delegated, or processed. The formalities and externals can."[4]

We all have a human tendency to overlook our weaknesses and rationalize our sub-par performance by the things that we do well. The church at Laodicea in Revelation 3:17 saw themselves as "rich, and increased with goods, and have need of nothing." God, however, saw them as "lukewarm" or mediocre and warns them that He is ready "to spue thee out of my mouth."

The next generation simply cannot afford to be raised by a generation of Laodicean leadership. I like the way Ronald Horton puts it when he says that Christian education must "bend its efforts to the end 'that the man of God may be perfect, throughly furnished unto all good works' (II Timothy 3:17)."[5] Recently, I had to ask myself: would the following paragraph describe me?

"Teachers of God's Word are unique. They are obligated to make a difference in the lives of learners. Their teaching should

---

[3] John W. Gardner, _Self-Renewal_, New York, NY, Harper & Row, 1964, pp. 131, 133.
[4] Ibid, p. 101.
[5] Ronald A. Horton, _Christian Education: Its Mandate and Mission_, Greenville, SC, Bob Jones University Press, 1992, p. 4.

have impact. They can never be content with status quo. They must continually engage learners in a quest for an ever-deeper understanding of and relationship with God. Teachers of the Word are uneasy with a Christianity of ease and success, or with faith that is culturally limited or anemic. Their role is to communicate undiluted, life-transforming principles. They are not content with anything less than to challenge learner growth. To teach Scripture is to be obliged to nurture lives that are increasingly conformed to the image of Christ."[6]

How can we escape the mire of mediocrity and set an example of excellence? We must recognize the three causes of mediocrity:

Our Education Exceeds Our Obedience

I love double-quarter pounders with cheese at McDonalds! It wouldn't matter what hot new item that franchise came up with – I would still order "# 4" – a double-quarter pounder with cheese, french fries, and a Diet Coke! (The Diet Coke makes me feel better about the whole thing.) I love those things. Now, I know that they're not good for my health. The fat calories are high, the red meat, etc., etc. But I don't care – I like 'em!

Now what's the problem? The problem is not my education – I am well aware of the harm that they could cause my health if I eat them too often – the problem is with my obedience. My education exceeds my obedience.

Spiritually, our young people today are filled with knowledge – after all, this is the "information age." It might astonish us to count up all of the Bible verses our kids have learned in Sunday school, vacation Bible school, at camp, and for Fine Arts competitions. But how many of these truths are they practicing on

---

[6] Dennis H. Dirks, *Christian Education: Foundations for the Future*, Chicago, IL, Moody Press, 1991, p. 137.

a daily basis in their lives? It was never God's intent that we simply have knowledge. Paul states that knowledge alone "puffeth up." (I Corinthians 8:1) A knowledge of the Gospel will not save anyone. King Agrippa in Acts 26 knew and believed the Gospel, but by his own testimony was not saved. Karl Marx is said to have had Matthew, Mark, Luke, and John memorized as a teenager, but died an atheist!

We simply cannot afford to content ourselves with teaching facts. James 1:22-25 makes it clear: "But be ye doers of the word, and not hearers only, deceiving your own selves. For if any be a hearer of the word, and not a doer, he is like unto a man beholding his natural face in a glass: For he beholdeth himself, and goeth his way, and straightway forgetteth what manner of man he was. But whoso looketh into the perfect law of liberty, and continueth therein, he being not a forgetful hearer, but a doer of the work, this man shall be blessed in his deed." In John 13:17, Jesus says: "If ye know these things, happy are ye if ye do them."

Revival will not come to our ranks when some preacher preaches something new – revival will come when God's people obey the old! The problem is not ignorance – the problem is disobedience. Our education exceeds our obedience. The need of the hour is not more decisions – the need of the hour is to start living the decisions we have already made. Until that happens, we will be plagued with mediocrity instead of progressing to maturity.

Our Past Excuses Our Present

Have you ever noticed that Satan always seems to talk in the past tense? As an "accuser of the brethren," he seems to have a pretty good memory. Countless times he thwarts our desire for excellence by reminding us of some sin in our past and convinces us that we are doomed to mediocrity as a result.

Satan may have had control of our lives in the past, but that does not mean he has to have a corner on our future! Have you ever stopped to consider that most of our Bible was written by murderers? Moses killed an Egyptian (Exodus 2:12), but later wrote the first five books of the Bible. David orchestrated the killing of Uriah (II Samuel 11:15), yet God used him to write the majority of the Psalms. The Apostle Paul, prior to his conversion, was responsible for the death of Stephen (Acts 7:58), and yet God used him to write the bulk of our New Testament Epistles. What a testimony these men are to the power of God over the past!

Romans 5:20 states: "Moreover the law entered, that the offence might abound. But where sin abounded, grace did much more abound." Now, the Romans may have thought, "We need more grace – so let's go sin some more so that we can have more grace, since the more sin there is, the more grace there will be." But Paul clearly diffuses that thinking two verses later in Romans 6:1-2: "What shall we say then? Shall we continue in sin, that grace may abound? God forbid." We don't need to sin in order to receive more grace. However, where there is sin – grace is always greater! Micah 7:18 says: "Who is a God like unto thee, that pardoneth iniquity, and passeth by the transgression of the remnant of his heritage? He retaineth not his anger for ever, because he delighteth in mercy." While Satan seeks to destroy us with our past, our heavenly Father delights in forgiving it!

Several years ago, I was enjoying great liberty in preaching at a summer teen camp. The young people listened attentively, the weather was gorgeous, the food was outstanding, the activities were superlative, but something was drastically wrong. Whenever I would give the invitation at the close of the services, it was like an invisible wall would go up. For the first three days of preaching there was absolutely no response. Needless to say, I was greatly concerned. One evening, as I was standing near the snack shop after the service, a group of about forty teens approached me. A young lady said, "Brother Goetsch, have you noticed that none of us are making any decisions?" I said, "Yes, I have." She said, "Would you like to know why?" I said, "Sure." Pointing to the others around her, she said, "Last year, all of us made a decision – but none of us kept them. So, this year, we aren't going to make any decisions." Immediately, I thought in my heart: The devil has these kids right where he wants them. He is defeating them in the present by something in the past! I'm glad they were honest, because with God's help and some teaching on how "a just man falleth seven times, and riseth up again," all but one of those teens made some kind of decision by the end of that week. A present excellence is being missed by excuses from the past!

Our Will is Being Exercised Instead of God's Will

Sadly, the Book of Judges closes with these words: "Every man did that which was right in his own eyes." Recently, I saw a license plate that read "LV 1 SLF" (Love one self). I'm sure the owner thought himself to be cutely innovative, but God said those words a long time ago in II Timothy 3:2: "For men shall be lovers of their own selves."

Isn't it amazing how we think that we know what is best for our lives. We make our plans to be successful, safe, and secure. We meticulously plot our course according to all the conventional wisdom of our day. We push ourselves to master the pinnacle of life, only to get there and find out we've lived for mediocrity. Our loftiest goal has come up short of God's desire for our lives, for He said, "For my thoughts are not your thoughts, neither are your ways my ways, saith the Lord. For as the heavens are higher than the earth, so are my ways higher than your ways, and my thoughts than your thoughts."(Isaiah 55:8-9).

For us to escape the average life of mediocrity and attain spiritual maturity, we must say with Christ, "for I do always those things that please him" (John 8:29). "Nevertheless not what I will, but what thou wilt" (Mark 14:36).

God has not called us to mentor mediocrity – He has called us to mentor others to maturity. That means we've got to be headed in that direction ourselves! The product can rise no higher than the pattern. Suppose that every young person God has given you to influence had the attitude of Ruth when she said to Naomi in Ruth 1:16: "Intreat me not to leave thee, or to return from following after thee: for whither thou goest, I will go; and where thou lodgest, I will lodge: thy people shall be my people, and thy God my God." Where will they end up? Who will be their people? What kind of God will they serve? With that kind of a challenge...

It is a sin to do less than our best. – Dr. Bob Jones Sr.

CHAPTER TWO

Edifying By Example

"In all things shewing thyself a pattern of good works." Titus 2:7

On Monday morning, January 18, 1982, Major Nonn Lowery led the Thunderbird precision flying team into a clear desert sky. The Air Force fighters broke from their usual diamond position to practice line abreast. Major Lowery, the "Boss," was flying # 1. At all times the other pilots fly in response to the "Boss." Major Dave Robinson (Pilot of # 2) says of the Boss: "He's my world – whether I'm right side up or upside down. It makes no difference where the ground is because my eyes are on the leader."

From the line abreast formation, the team began to execute the line abreast loop. At the top, all four planes were upside down and began to dive. Lowery pulled back on his stick to complete the loop, but a tiny piece of metal had come loose and prevented him from pulling out. The other pilots kept their eyes focused on the "Boss," as they had been trained. The four planes, in formation, slammed into the earth at 490 miles per hour. The pilots of #2, 3, and 4 never had a clue what was happening because their focus was completely on their leader. Even though they were in one of the most technologically advanced machines in existence, they were following a man."[1]

The responsibility of being a parent, pastor, or teacher is so much bigger than our "to do list," our day-timer, our computer, desk, pulpit, lectern, or kitchen table. Somebody has their eyes focused on you! You are the "boss" they are following. Young people are slamming into the world at high rates of speed to become spiritual fatalities today because of wrong examples in leadership.

It is impossible to separate the "teaching" from the "teacher" or the "message" from the "messenger." All instruction consists of truth and personality and one cannot be effective without the other. I highly doubt that you remember everything that you were taught in first grade, but I'll venture to say that you remember your teacher's name and could describe her in detail. Lynn Gannett states: "The saying 'more is caught than taught' proves to be true because teachers' attitudes about the Lord, the Bible, themselves, and students impact learning. Most adults have forgotten the details taught to them by their favorite teacher, but they have not forgotten the teacher. It has been said, 'First the student loves the teacher, then the student loves the teacher's Lord.'"[2]

Dennis Dirks makes a similar point: "Unless the teacher is stretching personally, there is less likelihood learners will also be stretched. . . . Teacher enthusiasm and excitement, when it is genuine, not conjured or faked, is a prime ingredient in promoting life change. Only when Scripture has passed through the grid of a

---

[1] Sermon Illustration

[2] Lynn Gannett, _Christian Education: Foundations for the Future_, Chicago, IL, Moody Press, 1991, pp. 116-117.

teacher's life is teaching with conviction possible. . . . What is taught must be matched by what is lived."[3]

Now, this is not to say that our curriculum is a non-factor in the process of education, but so much of what we are trying to accomplish in the lives of our students cannot be learned from a textbook, homework assignment, or laboratory experiment. The mentoring of a person must be done by a person. Ronald Horton has this to say: "The role of the teacher is essential in Christian education. The student needs a visible pattern of the goal toward which he is striving and a human instrument to assist him toward that goal. The goal consists of moral and spiritual as well as intellectual characteristics . . . qualities that can be communicated only by a person."[4] Harry Munro argued in his book "Protestant Nurture" that "the character and personality of the teacher have a more dominant effect on the lives of the student than the content of the lesson."[5]

The Apostle Paul makes several appeals to his followers to imitate his example. In Philippians 3:17 he says: "Brethren, be followers together of me, and mark them which walk so as ye have us for an ensample." Again, in Philippians 4:9, he invites: "Those things, which ye have both learned, and received, and heard, and seen in me, do: and the God of peace shall be with you." In I Corinthians 11:1 he boldly states: "Be ye followers of me, even as I also am of Christ."

This whole idea may scare us half to death. After all, who are we to put ourselves up on a pedestal and invite everyone to imitate

---

[3] Dennis H. Dirks, *Christian Education: Foundations for the Future*, Chicago, IL, Moody Press, 1991 p. 153.

[4] Ronald A. Horton, *Christian Education: Its Mandate and Mission*, Greenville, SC, Bob Jones University Press, 1992, p. 16.

[5] Perry G. Downs, *Teaching for Spiritual Growth*, Grand Rapids, MI, Zondervan, 1994, p. 159.

us? I like what Lawrence Richards has said: "We are to be examples. . . not of perfection, but of a process. We can afford to remove the veils because we are being transformed: progress is being made. . . . We are to be models with whom others can identify. Strikingly, it is our weaknesses rather than our strengths that most help others see themselves like us."[6] Or, as Perry Downs reminds us: "God has called us, not to model perfection, but to model redemption. We are to be living demonstrations, not of how good we are, but of how good God is."[7]

The stakes are too high for us to have mechanical failure in the cockpit of our homes, churches, and schools. We must take the challenge of edifying through example in at least three crucial areas.

An Example of Character

Richard C. Cabot, the leader of Harvard in 1900 said: "If there is not an education of purpose; if there is no ethical basis for education; then the more we know, the livelier crooks and smarter villains we will become." What a prophetic statement that has become. Throughout the twentieth century, education increased in every aspect, and yet somewhere along the way, we forgot to teach character. We produced an education without ethics so that now one does not need a gun to rob a bank, but rather a laptop. Benjamin Mays, the distinguished black leader of Moorehouse College, used to say, "My aim is not to turn out preachers, or doctors, or lawyers. My goal is to turn out men!"

Character cannot be microwaved. There is no drive-thru window where character can be purchased on the run. Character

---

[6] Lawrence O. Richards, *Christian Education*, Grand Rapids, MI, Zondervan, 1975, p. 142.
[7] Downs, p. 164.

101 cannot be taken via correspondence school. Character must be observed from every angle under the microscope of daily living. The best content in the world will fall on deaf ears when character is absent. Dr. Bruce Wilkinson says: "Character will always control the content – eventually. When the Spirit of God is quenched and sin is given free reign, not only will the Spirit not be present in the teaching, but soon neither will the Scriptures. The teacher or preacher will begin to shape the content to match his lifestyle."[8]

Think about what Paul admonishes young Timothy to be an example of in I Timothy 4:12: "Let no man despise thy youth; but be thou an example of the believers, in word, in conversation, in charity, in spirit, in faith, in purity." He is speaking of character traits, is he not? And doesn't Peter likewise admonish us in II Peter 1:5-7 to add character to our faith? "And beside this, giving all diligence, add to your faith virtue; and to virtue knowledge; And to knowledge temperance; and to temperance patience; and to patience godliness; And to godliness brotherly kindness; and to brotherly kindness charity." The world would tell us that character doesn't matter – performance is the only thing that is important. But God goes on to tell us that the only way to have proper performance is to have proper character: "For if these things be in you, and abound, they make you that ye shall neither be barren nor unfruitful in the knowledge of our Lord Jesus Christ. But he that lacketh these things is blind, and cannot see afar off, and hath forgotten that he was purged from his old sins." (II Peter 1:8-9)

Someone once said, "Your sermon preaches but an hour – your life preaches all the week." Benjamin Harvey Hill said of Robert E. Lee: "He was a foe without hate, a friend without

[8] Bruce Wilkinson, *The Seven Laws of the Learner*, Sisters, OR, Multnomah Press, 1992, p. 39.

treachery, a soldier without cruelty. . . . He was a public officer without vices, a neighbor without reproach, a Christian without hypocrisy, a man without guile." No wonder his life is still teaching!

How long will you be impacting lives? Long after the sermon is forgotten, and the lesson notes are lost, will the example of your character still linger in the hearts of your followers? Dr. Wilkinson states: "When I ask adults to select the teacher who most influenced them, it is always the one who had the most noble character and commitment. Those teachers usually were not the easiest nor the hardest in the classroom, but something about them aroused a genuine respect and admiration. We, their students, wished that someday we could be like them."[9]

An Example of Courage

Christianity is no longer marked by a courageous zeal, but rather by a comfort zone! Too often today, as leaders, our minds are focused on our days off, vacation pay, pension plans, and perks rather than on our call to mentorship. No wonder then that our young people are deaf to the call of God upon their lives for the ministry. Why should they walk by faith when their mentors walk by sight? Why should they take a risk when their mentors talk of reason? Why should they be willing to sacrifice when their mentors want only success?

The hall of faith needs some new portraits! Have you ever read Hebrews 11? Not one thing in that chapter done by any of those men or women makes common sense. But they are all listed there because of one thing – FAITH! When are we going to stop trying to figure everything out about the will of God, and step out by faith and take some risks? The minute we get it figured out, it

---

[9] Ibid.

16

ceases to be faith, for "faith is the substance of things hoped for, the evidence of things not seen." (Hebrews 11:1) Regardless of how successful our ministry is perceived to be by others, it is unnoticed by God if it can be done without faith. "But without faith it is impossible to please him." (Hebrews 11:6) In fact, if you or I are doing anything in our ministry that does not require faith – risk – courage, it is SIN! "For whatsoever is not of faith is sin." (Romans 14:23)

Alexander Solzhenitsyn, in his Harvard commencement address on June 8, 1978, said, "Must one point out that from ancient times a decline in courage has been considered the beginning of the end?" No wonder the wasting harvest fields cry for laborers today! Oh, let's put courage back in the curriculum. Let's mix faith in with the facts and add an "R" to the three we already teach – let's teach our young people about "risking" their lives for the cause of Christ! We can't just "talk" about it – we've got to "walk" it. The Bible doesn't say "we talk by faith" – it says "we walk by faith."

An Example of Commitment

A generation of quitters today is raising a generation of young people that won't even try. Divorced parents have raised children that live together with the opposite sex without bothering to get married. Adults who have quit church have now raised a generation of atheists and agnostics. In an increasingly hostile culture toward Christianity, our young people desperately need examples of commitment to Christ.

It seems today that the smallest obstacle, the slightest criticism, the unpraised work, or the unnoticed sacrifice causes us to throw in the towel and quit. The level of our commitment is based on the extrinsic rewards rather than the intrinsic responsibilities.

Recently, my heart was drawn to a story on the front page of the *USA Today* newspaper entitled: "Devotion, Desire Drive Youths to Martyrdom." It read in part: The Hotaris are preparing for a party to celebrate the killing of 21 Israelis this month by their son, a suicide bomber. . . . "I am very happy and proud of what my son did, and frankly, am a bit jealous," says Hassan Hotari, 54, father of the young man who carried out the attack June 1 outside a disco in Tel Aviv. It was Israel's worst suicide bombing in nearly four years. "I wish I had done [the bombing]. My son has fulfilled the Prophet's [Mohammed's] wishes. He has become a hero! Tell me, what more could a father ask?"

Lured by promises of financial stability for their families, eternal martyrdom and unlimited sex in the afterlife, dozens of militant Palestinians like Hotari aspire to blow themselves up, Israeli and Palestinian officials say. Their goal: to kill or injure as many Jews as possible in the hope that Israel will withdraw from Gaza and the West Bank.

At any time, Israeli officials believe, Hamas has from five to 20 men, ages 18 to 23, awaiting orders to carry out suicide attacks. The group also claims to have "tens of thousands" of youths ready to follow in their footsteps. "We like to grow them," Yosef says, "from kindergarten through college." In Hamas-run kindergartens, signs on the walls read: "The children of the kindergarten are the "shaeeds" (holy martyrs) of tomorrow." At an Islamic school in Gaza City run by Hamas, 11-year-old Palestinian student Ahmed's small frame and boyish smile are deceiving. They mask a determination to kill at any cost. "I will make my body a bomb that will blast the flesh of Zionists, the sons of pigs and monkeys,"

Ahmed says. "I will tear their bodies into little pieces and cause them more pain than they will ever know."

They join because of their absolute devotion to God and their desire to die with Jewish blood on their hands. It's not a heroic thing, it's a holy thing. A would-be bomber is selected for his mission only days, sometimes hours, before it is to occur, Israeli officials say. As part of the preparation, the recruit is taken to a cemetery, where he is told to prepare for death by lying between gravesites for hours. He wears a white, hooded shroud normally used to cover bodies for burial. The recruit is then taken to a safe house. A video is made in which he states his consent to become a suicide bomber and his devotion to Islam. It will be played for the public after his death. A still photograph is taken that will be reproduced and displayed through the West Bank and Gaza to honor him after death.

Because secrecy is paramount, Hamas leaders will not allow the recruit to say goodbye to his family or tell them his plans. Meanwhile, separate Hamas groups already have selected the target, constructed the bomb that will be attached to the recruit's belt, and started preparations to get him to the site.

On June 1, it was Hotari's turn. Israeli officials, quoting eyewitnesses, say two Hamas operatives drove him to the Dolphin Disco in Tel Aviv, a popular club often packed with Russian immigrant teenagers. They said Hotari slipped unnoticed into line and positioned himself among several girls. Then, while flirting with one of the girls, Hotari triggered the explosives. The blast was so intense that it tore limbs from the victims' bodies, scattered flesh up to six blocks away, and vaporized Hotari and the girl next to him. It killed 21 people, in addition to Hotari, and injured nearly 100.

Now, nearly 30 days later, his parents are preparing to mark the anniversary of his death as devout Muslims often do. "My prayer is that Saeed's brothers, friends, and fellow Palestinians will sacrifice their lives, too," Hotari's father says. "There is no better way to show God you love him."[10]

Here is a young boy, proclaimed as an example of heroism by his own family because of his commitment. And did you notice – tens of thousands of others wait to follow his example!

Do we really believe that our God is the true God? If so, why is our commitment so shallow and temporary? He is not asking us to blow ourselves up in death as an example of our commitment – He simply asks us to "live" a life of commitment to Him. And perhaps if we did, there would be "tens of thousands" waiting to follow our example! Paul summed it up nicely: "For to me to live is Christ. . ." (Philippians 1:21)

"You have to be different to make a difference. You cannot change anything by adding more of the same."[11]

---

[10]USA Today, Tuesday, June 26, 2001, pp. 1-2.

[11] Jim Berg, *Changed into His Image,* Greenville, SC, Bob Jones University Press, 1999, p. 211

CHAPTER THREE

Communicating Through Consistency

"The scribes and Pharisees sit in Moses' seat: All therefore whatsoever they bid you observe, that observe and do; but do not ye after their works: for they say, and do not." Matthew 23:2-3

In 1973, L. M. "Lem" Clymer was named president of Holiday Inns, Inc. During the decade of the 1970's, he was widely acclaimed as having restored prestige and profitability to the Holiday Inns hotel chain after it had suffered a period of decline. In 1977, while he was at the apex of his career with Holiday Inns, Clymer stunned the business world when he abruptly resigned his position. His reason: The board of directors had approved, over his objection, the construction of a $55 million hotel-casino in Atlantic City.

Ron Lee Davis tells how that only a few months after his resignation, he and his wife had dinner in Memphis with Lem and his wife. Over dinner, Clymer explained that his motive for resigning was his love for Jesus Christ. "I had a vision of Holiday Inns," he said, "as a chain of family hotels. My desire for the company was that whenever people heard the name Holiday Inn, they would know it was a place where parents and kids could go for fun and relaxation, free of the sordid environment that always surrounds a casino. The board of Holiday Inns didn't share my vision, and they voted for the casino."

"It must have been a hard decision," Davis said.

"Hard?" He seemed genuinely surprised by the comment, as if it had never occurred to him to make any decision other than the one he made. "No, Ron, it wasn't hard at all. I knew what the Lord wanted me to do. It was all I could do. Not that I feel any resentment toward the board. They were just doing what they felt was best for the company and the shareholders. But I couldn't be a part of that decision. I couldn't do that and still maintain my own integrity."

Davis goes on to say: "There's no such thing in this world as cheap integrity. Integrity is absolute. And integrity has a price. To have integrity is to be the same person you are alone, when no one is watching, as you are in the glare of the spotlight. As Howard Hendricks put it, 'You show me a leader who is great in public and I will show you a leader who is even greater in private.' That means that your secret inner self is seamlessly joined to your outer self. And that's very hard. . . . But to live any other way is to live a lie."[1]

If there is one thing that young people do not tolerate – it's hypocrisy! They'll watch you and test you, and when they sense anything close to phoniness they will run from you. On the other hand, talent and personality will never draw people to follow us like consistency of life will. Why did young Timothy pay such careful attention to the aged Apostle Paul? Because when Paul

---

[1] Ron Lee Davis, *Mentoring: The Strategy of the Master*, Nashville, TN, Thomas Nelson, 1991, pp. 102-103.

admonished him to "exercise thyself rather unto godliness" (I Timothy 4:7), Timothy's mind flashed back to an earlier statement of his mentor about his own life: "And herein do I exercise myself, to have always a conscience void of offence toward God, and toward men." (Acts 24:16) You see, the life of the mentor matched the lesson of the mentor.

The sons-in-law of Lot reacted differently to their father's warning to flee Sodom. Genesis 19:14 says: "But he seemed as one that mocked unto his sons in law." The practice of Lot had not matched the preaching of Lot, and as a result, those that he should have been mentoring – perished.

Paul doesn't mince any words about this matter in Romans 2:21-22: "Thou therefore which teachest another, teachest thou not thyself? Thou that preachest a man should not steal, dost thou steal? Thou that sayest a man should not commit adultery, dost thou commit adultery? Thou that abhorrest idols, dost thou commit sacrilege?" And then he adds the sad note in verse 24: "For the name of God is blasphemed among the Gentiles through you, as it is written."

T. S. Henderson states: "Practice and precept ought to be in harmony; and we must seek to make them so, not by restraining our voice from the utterance of the latter, but by redoubling our attention to the former. . . . In any Christian it [inconsistency] is an evil of untold magnitude, but in one who professes to teach Christianity, its turpitude must be ten times greater. Drunkenness is a dreadful vice in any man; but do we not justly reckon it a thing of greater heinousness, and more fearful danger, when detected in a sentinel on duty, or in the driver of a railway engine, with the lives of many a score depending on his punctuality and care? So of the teacher. If any man could perish alone in his iniquity, he cannot. If the light that he professes to hold forth is transmitted through an impure atmosphere, he but renders the darkness more visible, and misleads where he pretends to guide. Of inconsistent teachers we learn something in the book of Proverbs, where in four short verses, we are told how useless is their work, and how halting their progress, how unsuitable their elevation to office, and how great, though often unperceived, the injury to themselves. "He that sendeth a message by the hand of a fool cutteth off the feet, and drinketh damage. The legs of the lame are not equal: so is a parable in the mouth of fools. As he that bindeth a stone in a sling, so is he that giveth honour to a fool. As a thorn goeth up into the hand of a drunkard, so is a parable in the mouth of fools." (Proverbs 26:6-9)[2]

To say that it is important to be consistent in one area over another would in itself be inconsistent. However, there are three areas especially important to youth if we are going to be successful at "communicating through consistency."

Consistently Honest

A man sat through a church service, and then on the way home, he fussed about the sermon, he fussed about the traffic, he fussed about the heat, and he fussed about the lateness of the meal being served. Then he bowed and prayed. His son was watching him all the way through this post-church experience. Just as they were beginning to pass the food he said, "Daddy, did God hear you when we left the church and you started fussin' about the sermon and about the traffic and about the heat?" The father sort of blushed and said, "Well, yes, son, He heard me." "Well, Daddy, did God hear you when you just prayed for this food right now?"

---

[2]T. S. Henderson, _The Good Teacher_, Philadelphia, PA, American Baptist Publication Society, (No date printed), pp. 36, 40-41.

24

The Dad said, "Well, yes, son, He. . . He. . . He heard me." "So, well, Daddy, which one did God believe?"[3]

We laugh at that little story, but it happens all too often. Sometimes it seems to us that kids never listen to us. But be dishonest just once and you'll find out they have been listening all along. Scripture teaches us that we are to be "speaking the truth" (Ephesians 4:15), while at the same time we are to be "in all things willing to live honestly" (Hebrews 13:18). In verse 4 of III John, John says: "I have no greater joy than to hear that my children walk in truth." In his commentary on that verse, John R. W. Stott, makes these comments: "To walk in truth is more than to give assent to it. It means to apply it to one's behavior. He who 'walks in the truth' is an integrated Christian in whom there is no dichotomy between profession and practice. On the contrary, there is in him an exact correspondence between his creed and his conduct. Such conformity of life to the truth on the part of his children brought John greater joy than anything else. To him truth mattered."

Jesus saved His most scathing message for the hypocrites. He called the Pharisees "blind leaders of the blind" and "whited sepulchres." The outside trappings were clean and righteous, but within they were filled with "extortion and excess, dead men's bones and all uncleanness." He called them "serpents" and "a generation of vipers." (Matthew 23:25-33) Hypocrisy is a horrible disease that leaves its victims paralyzed by doubt! To communicate consistency to those following us, we must shorten our creeds and lengthen our deeds!

Charles H. Spurgeon, Baptist minister of London, England, had a pastor-friend, Dr. Newman Hall, who wrote a book entitled

---

[3] Charles R. Swindoll, *The Tale of the Tardy Oxcart*, Nashville, TN, Word Publishing, 1998, p. 285.

Come to Jesus. Another preacher published an article in which he ridiculed Hall, who bore it patiently for a little while. But when the article gained popularity, Hall sat down and wrote a letter of protest. His answer was full of retaliatory invectives that outdid anything in the article which had attacked him. Before mailing the letter, Hall took it to Spurgeon for his opinion.

Spurgeon read it carefully, and then, handing it back, asserted it was excellent and that the writer of the article deserved it all. "But," he added, "it just lacks one thing." After a pause Spurgeon continued, "Underneath your signature you ought to write the words, 'Author of - Come to Jesus.'"

The two godly men looked at each other for a few moments. Then Hall tore the letter to shreds.[4]

Consistently Humble

On the one hand we tell our followers that Christ is our only hope – our only Savior. That without Him – we are nothing. That we can do all things only "through" Christ Who strengthens us. But then they listen to us boast of our accomplishments, making ourselves the hero of every illustration, and reveling in the praise that is heaped upon us.

Robert Morrison of China wrote: "The great fault, I think, with our mission is that no one likes to be second." Great things could be accomplished today if we would just forget about who gets the credit. Solomon in Proverbs 20:6 gives us the reality of the matter: "Most men will proclaim every one his own goodness" but later admonishes us in chapter 27 and verse 2: "Let another man praise thee, and not thine own mouth; a stranger, and not thine own lips."

---

[4] Ibid, p. 41.

This is where the ministry differs from the secular world. Success in the business world is determined by how close to the top your name appears on the organizational flow chart. Climbing the ladder becomes the goal, and the executive chair is where everyone in the company desires to ultimately sit. But the ministry is no place to be analyzing how many people are over or under you, or whether you'll be moving to an office with a window soon. Jesus addressed this very issue in Matthew 20:25-28: "Ye know that the princes of the Gentiles exercise dominion over them, and they that are great exercise authority upon them. But it shall not be so among you: but whosoever will be great among you, let him be your minister; And whosoever will be chief among you, let him be your servant: Even as the Son of man came not to be ministered unto, but to minister, and to give his life a ransom for many."

Leroy Eims makes the following comments about this matter: "There is always room for one more servant. The small area in the spotlight can get a bit crowded, but there is always room in the shadows for the person who is eager to serve."

Stephen was a man full of faith and power, and the enemies of Christ were not able to resist the wisdom and the spirit by which he spoke. He had a remarkable grasp of the Word of God and the boldness to preach it with conviction. One day the apostles came to him and asked if he would serve tables for some Grecian widows who were being neglected in the daily distribution of food.

Stephen could have said, "Me? Serve tables? Apparently you are unaware of my wisdom, power, faith, and preaching ability. Get someone else to stand in the shadows and serve. I'm sure you can see that I am better suited to the spotlight in center stage."

But no, thank God, that was not his reaction. He eagerly took his place among the six other servants and waited on tables. I'm sure that is one of the prime reasons he has held a place in God's spotlight down through the centuries. Only one person could be the first martyr in the cause of Christ and Stephen is it. No one can ever replace him."[5]

"He must increase, but I must decrease" (John 3:30). ". . . And be clothed with humility: for God resisteth the proud, and giveth grace to the humble. Humble yourselves therefore under the mighty hand of God, that he may exalt you in due time" (I Peter 5:5-6) Truly, the way up in mentorship is down!

Consistently Holy

Only the attribute of holiness is raised to the level of "triple pronouncement." R. C. Sproul observes: "Only once in sacred Scripture is an attribute of God elevated to the third degree. . . . Only once is a characteristic of God mentioned three times in succession. The Bible says that God is holy, holy, holy. . . . The Bible never says that God is love, love, love, or mercy, mercy, mercy, or wrath, wrath, wrath, or justice, justice, justice. It does say that He is holy, holy, holy, the whole earth is full of His glory."[6]

Unfortunately, in our day, there is little emphasis on the holiness of God, and as a result, there is little evidence of holy living in our lives. Perry Downs states: "It is striking to contrast the Old Testament's strict guidelines for approaching God with the rather casual and almost cavalier ways people approach him today. In some contemporary worship, there is almost no sense that God is holy, that He is to be revered and feared because of His terrible holiness. Rather, the tame God of some Christians can be approached in any way and with any attitude they desire. As a

---

[5] Leroy Eims, *Be The Leader You Were Meant To Be*, Wheaton, IL, Victor Books, 1976, p. 42.
[6] R. C. Sproul, *The Holiness of God*, Wheaton, IL, Tyndale House, 1985, p. 40.

result they are unimpressed with God and see Him as almost incidental to their daily lives. Focus turns to self. Happiness and fulfillment become all-consuming, and the Biblical calls to deny ourselves and follow God are only faintly heard."[7]

Today, the cries of "legalism" and "narrow-mindedness" and "too many rules" are heard particularly from our youth. We want liberty and freedom to express ourselves as we please without any boundaries. Our culture doesn't help as the lines between right and wrong, good and evil, bitter and sweet, have been rubbed out long ago. As Isaiah put it: "And judgment is turned away backward, and justice standeth afar off: for truth is fallen in the street, and equity cannot enter." (Isaiah 59:14)

But while culture changes – Christ hasn't! "Jesus Christ the same yesterday, to day, and for ever." (Hebrews 13:8) And His command in I Peter 1:14-16 still stands: "As obedient children, not fashioning yourselves according to the former lusts in your ignorance: But as he which hath called you is holy, so be ye holy in all manner of conversation; Because it is written, Be ye holy; for I am holy."

Now this is where it really gets tough because often our followers are looking for that loophole to let them off the hook. If they can find one inconsistency in our walk, it will excuse their sin. Remember though, we are not modeling "perfection" (Christ was the only Person capable of that), we are modeling "redemption." Do our children see us becoming more like Christ or more like the world? Do our students see us growing into Christ's likeness as the school year progresses? What changes do the teenagers see in your life for God since they entered the youth group? Those are fair questions!

---

[7] Perry G. Downs, *Teaching for Spiritual Growth*, Grand Rapids, MI, Zondervan, 1994, p. 47.

Sure, we'll mess up – but our followers can more readily identify with our failures than they can with our successes. So admit the failure and grow from it in such a way as to communicate a consistent walk with the Lord. Young people don't have to look far to see hypocrisy, fraud, deceit, guile, double-mindedness, and two-facedness, "but a faithful man who can find? (Proverbs 20:6)

In conclusion, listen to what T. S. Henderson says about this matter of consistency: "Let it not be imagined that the inconsistencies of teachers are productive of evil only when they are gross in their nature, and public in their notoriety. The teacher is at all times more closely watched than he is aware of. It may be that his every look is noted. The thoughtless act of levity, the passing expression of discontent, the muttered accents of pride, the gorgeous trappings of vanity, the evasive words that cloak a falsehood, the selfish indulgence of sloth, the foolish emulation of rivalry, the pettish explosions of envy, the fretful gesture of impatience, may go further than we suspect to neutralize the influence of our teachings."[8]

"A minister's life is the life of his ministry." - Archbishop Leighton

"The sins of teachers are the teachers of sin." - Ralph Venning

---

[8]Henderson, p. 44.

CHAPTER FOUR

Leadership through Love

"And on some have compassion, making a difference." Jude 22

In chapter one, we discussed the need to escape the mire of mediocrity and strive to be an example of excellence in this ministry of mentoring. The Apostle Paul pens a lengthy portion of Scripture on the various gifts that God has given to the body of Christ in I Corinthians 12. As he closes the chapter, he states: "But covet earnestly the best gifts: and yet I shew unto you a more excellent way." He then begins chapter 13 by showing us that these gifts, though they are wonderful and very necessary, are nothing without love! "Though I speak with the tongues of men and of angels, and have not charity, I am become as sounding brass, or a tinkling cymbal. And though I have the gift of prophecy, and understand all mysteries, and all knowledge; and though I have all faith, so that I could remove mountains, and have not charity, I am nothing. And though I bestow all my goods to feed the poor, and though I give my body to be burned, and have not charity, it profiteth me nothing."

I hope you didn't read through those familiar verses too fast. Did you notice what the Holy Spirit said? If you could teach like the angel Gabriel, and if you understood every passage of the Bible and could exegete it perfectly in a sermon, and if you had enough faith to move the Rocky Mountains to Kansas, and if you gave every dime of your income away to the poor, and when you were eighty years old you willingly went to the stake to be burned in martyrdom, it would be absolutely worthless and count for nothing with God, if it wasn't done in love! I guess that makes this chapter pretty important.

It's easy to lose our passion in the ministry today. We've been trained, we have an abundance of tools, no one expects any miracles to happen, anyway – it's easy to put in our time, fulfill our requirements, and become professional. We are "doing the will of God". . . but not "from the heart." (Ephesians 6:6) Perry Downs puts it straight-forward to the teacher: "The heart of the Christian educator must be motivated by love. While no one has absolutely pure motivation, still it must be the growing desire of our hearts to see people maturing in their faith. Our educational ministry must not be self-serving, but rather an act of service to others. Teaching should be presented as a gift of love to others."[1]

Carl Sandberg on February 12, 1959 gave a description of Abraham Lincoln entitled "Steel and Velvet." Ron Lee Davis takes this same title and applies it in the following article to the Lord Jesus Christ:

A man of steel, Jesus confronted the religious evil of his day. He called the corrupt religious leaders vipers, hypocrites, white-washed tombs full of dead bones. Like steel, he cleared the money-changers out of the Temple. Like steel, he confronted

---

[1] Perry G. Downs, _Teaching for Spiritual Growth_, Grand Rapids, MI, Zondervan, 1994, p. 16.

Peter, told him he could be a rock, that he should be consistent, that he should stop wavering.

Yet it was a man of velvet who wept over the death of his friend Lazarus. It was the velvet in the man that gave him compassion for the woman caught in adultery. It was the velvet in him that led him to reach out to the little children who crowded around him. It was the velvet in him that compelled him, just hours before the Cross, to kneel before his disciples and wash their feet.

Davis goes on to make the following application: Our task as mentors is to imitate the Master Mentor, Jesus himself. Our lives must be marked both with Christ's toughness and his tenderness, both his steel and his velvet. This means that those of us who are tender Christians will have to become a bit more tough, and those of us who are tough will have to learn a little more tenderness.

The tender Christian who avoids building toughness into his or her life soon becomes little more than a weak sentimentalist. The tough Christian who has no use for tenderness inevitably hardens into a harshly critical Pharisee. To be Christ-like mentors, we must have these complementary qualities in dynamic balance in our lives.

If we are to be conformed into the image of Christ, we must allow Christ to mold and reshape our character. We must invite him to put a reinforcing rod of steel into our backbone so that we can live out his strength. We must allow him to reupholster our hard surfaces and rough edges with velvet so that we can live out his love and compassion.[2]

---

[2] Ron Lee Davis, *Mentoring: The Strategy of the Master*, Nashville, TN, Thomas Nelson, 1991, p. 84.

Our world is certainly not short on "talk" when it comes to love – but what kind of love is needed in this mentoring process? What kind of charity saturates this "more excellent way" and that "makes a difference"?

A Sensitive Love

Years ago, the pastor of a fair-sized church had a huge problem – a Sunday School class of seventh grade boys! This group of Junior-highers had terrorized several teachers and the word was out – no one wanted to teach this class. The pastor prayed earnestly for a teacher and scanned the membership list in desperation – surely there had to be someone that could take this class. One morning, he was reminded of a man shaking his hand some months before and volunteering to do anything the pastor might need. However, he was a relatively new Christian and had never been trained to teach. Besides, he was introverted and not very good with words. But the pastor couldn't seem to get this man out of his mind.

He hated to ask him, but there were no other options. The man was shocked by his pastor's request, and expressed his unworthiness and inadequacy, but agreed to give it a try with the Lord's help. The church and pastor watched carefully, hoping that these ruthless young boys would not destroy the faith of this inexperienced and untrained teacher. To their shock and amazement, the class began to grow! The boys eagerly came with their lessons completed, Bibles in hand, memory verses ready to recite. Their voices filled the entire Sunday school wing as they sang the choruses each week. One Sunday, the Pastor stood outside the door and listened as the teacher weakly stumbled through the Bible lesson while the boys sat in rapt attention.

That morning, after the service, the pastor called the Sunday School teacher into his office. He expressed his amazement at the fine job he was doing and inquired of him what it was that had made such a difference in these young lives. The teacher shrugged and offered no explanation. As the Pastor continued to probe, he noticed the man held in his lap a small black notebook along with his Bible. The Pastor asked if he might take a look at this "lesson book." Reluctantly, the man obliged. As the cover was turned back, each page was dedicated to one of those seventh grade boys. There was a photograph taped in the upper right hand corner with a name beneath it. Then neatly listed on the page were addresses, phone numbers, the name of each boy's school, their parent's names, their hobbies, and their favorite candy. The pages were brittle as the pastor turned them, soaked in the tears of their praying Sunday school teacher, who had overcome their mischievousness and hardened hearts, not with skill or knowledge, but with love!

Colossians 3:14 says: "And above all things put on charity, which is the bond of perfectness." Interestingly, the word "perfectness" means "maturity" here. Remember the goal of our ministry? Maturity! And here is the bond or glue that holds everything else we do together – Love! Do you know what it means to a little bus child when you remember him by name the second time he comes to Sunday school? Do you know what it means to a third grader who gets a "Good Job" from his teacher on the top of his homework paper or maybe even a sticker? Do you know what it means to a teenager when you ask him how his game went last night or how his job is going? It's called sensitive love.

Paul Tournier, the Swiss Christian psychologist who has been a tender-tough mentor to hundreds of people around the world, was interviewed a few years ago. When the interviewer asked him to explain his counseling techniques, Tournier replied, "It's a little embarrassing for me, having all these students coming from all over the world to study my techniques, for they always go away disappointed. All I have learned to do is simply accept people right in the midst of their struggles."[3]

How hard is that? The very minimum we should do as mentors for those following us, is to guarantee, that we are there for them, that we will unconditionally accept and love them. (By the way, I believe that's the guarantee God has given us.)

A Sacrificial Love

Need we say much here? "Greater love hath no man than this, that a man lay down his life for his friends." (John 15:13) No greater sacrifice of love has ever been made than when "Christ died for us." (Romans 5:8) The Apostle Paul expressed his desire to show this kind of sacrificial love in Romans 9:3 when he cries: "For I could wish that myself were accursed from Christ for my brethren, my kinsmen according to the flesh."

God did not require Paul to die in sacrificial love for others, but He did allow him to live in sacrificial love for others – "Therefore watch, and remember, that by the space of three years, I ceased not to warn every one night and day with tears." (Acts 20:31) "I will very gladly spend and be spent for you. . ." (II Corinthians 12:15)

Are we willing to sacrifice anything in order to love in this mentoring process? Young people need us to be available more than they need our answers. They need time as much as they need truth, and our concern as much as our curriculum. Are you willing to give up your Saturday golf game or your Sunday afternoon nap to mentor some kid?

---

[3] Ibid, p. 75.

It was a Wednesday night not long after a horrible accident involving three of our college young ladies. The dozens of people who had been praying in the hospital lobby had moved to the church for the evening service, and I was asked to stay at the hospital with Jessica's dad. My emotions and energy had long been spent as we had girls in two different hospitals fifty miles apart. After spending some time on our knees in prayer, Mr. Downey invited me back with him to that Intensive Care Unit where his daughter, in a coma, struggled between life and death. This godly, faithful man, who had lost his first wife in a similar car accident several years before, leaned up against that hospital wall and through rivers of tears begged God for His strength, mercy, and grace. I never felt so helpless in my life. I couldn't seem to think of any appropriate Scripture – no words of comfort came to my mind. Finally, I slipped my arm around John's neck, and I said, "Brother Downey, I don't know what to say, but I'm here to cry with you." As he buried his face in my shoulder, I'll never forget his words: "Thanks, Brother Goetsch, that's all I need."

Whenever I see Jessica now and her family, who were not made bitter by trial but rather better, I think – what could have been more important for me to do during those days, than to be there for them? Is someone in your care hurting today? Could someone use a little time, a kind note or deed? Sure, it will cost you something – but we're called to mentor – and that requires "Sacrificial Love."

Selfless Love

The ministry has nothing to do with "getting," but it has everything to do with "giving." If you are in this thing for what you can attain – get out now! T. S. Henderson makes this point quite clear:

But none may think that he who enters on the work. . . will have nothing to endure. Let him try, and he will discover it to be otherwise. He must not be a feather-bed soldier, nor may he deem his a mere summer campaign. He will have to rouse himself from his slumbers in the morning. He will have to take, oftentimes, a hurried meal. He will have to face the weather, however inclement. He will have to fight against all physical, if not also at times against mental disinclination to his task. The bodily rest will have to be foregone, which is the gracious Sabbath privilege allowed for the Christian's personal refreshment; and to others must be devoted many an hour which he could find it in his heart gladly to spend in private communion with God. When any of these considerations weigh heavily on the mind of the toil-worn laborer, nothing can revive his drooping energies, save the sustaining grace of God from without, and the impelling principle of a heaven-kindled zeal within. He must be able to say, "The zeal of thine house – of thy church – of thy cause – hath eaten me up." He must be one who studies not to please himself. He must learn to say, with his Master, "I have meat to eat that ye know not of; I must work the works of him that sent me while it is day. Now is my soul troubled, and what shall I say? Father, save me from this hour? Father, glorify thy name." His motto must be, "Not to be ministered unto, but to minister;" his rule, "Let no man seek his own, but every man another's wealth;" his principle of action, "Not seeking mine own profit, but the profit of many, that they may be saved."[4]

Are you "crucified with Christ"? Have you died to self? Paul stated: "I will very gladly spend and be spent for you; though the more abundantly I love you, the less I be loved." (II Corinthians

---

[4] T. S. Henderson, _The Good Teacher_, Philadelphia, PA, American Baptist Publication Society, (No date printed), pp. 105-107.

12:15) The love that Paul received back from those he mentored didn't match the love he had put in. But for him, it didn't matter. Why? Because he was dead – dead to self!

When I read the following little story, it not only stirred the emotions of my heart, but also caused me to reevaluate my motives of love in the ministry.

Little Chad was a shy, quiet young fella. One day he came home and told his mother, he'd like to make a valentine for everyone in his class. Her heart sank. She thought, "I wish he wouldn't do that!" because she watched the children when they walked home from school. Her Chad was always behind them. They laughed and hung on to each other and talked to each other. But Chad was never included. Nevertheless, she decided to go along with her son. So she purchased the paper and glue and crayons. For three whole weeks, night after night, Chad painstakingly made thirty-five valentines.

Valentine's Day dawned and Chad was beside himself with excitement! He carefully stacked them up, put them in a bag, and bolted out the door. His mom decided to bake him his favorite cookies and serve them up warm and nice with a cool glass of milk when he came home from school. She just knew he'd be disappointed; maybe that would ease the pain a little. It hurt her to think that he wouldn't get many valentines – maybe none at all.

That afternoon she had the cookies and the milk out on the table. When she heard the children outside, she looked out the window. Sure enough here they came, laughing and having the best time. And, as always, there was Chad in the rear. He walked a little faster than usual. She fully expected him to burst into tears as soon as he got inside. His arms were empty, she noticed, and when the door opened she choked back the tears.

"Mommy has some warm cookies and milk for you."

But he hardly heard her words. He just marched right on by, his face aglow, and all he could say was:

"Not a one . . . not a one."

Her heart sank.

And then he added, "I didn't forget a one, not a single one!"[5]

Whew! Is our love for those that God has entrusted to us to mentor that sensitive, sacrificial, and selfless? Is your leadership being questioned or ignored? – "Charity never faileth." (I Corinthians 13:8)

As a junior high boy, I thought I had arrived. I was taller than my mom, was playing on all the sports teams, and was a part of the "in-crowd" at school. I had decided that I didn't need anyone telling me what to do – I could take care of myself.

I don't recall how it all started, but one night upon arrival home from school, I got into an argument with my mom. Dad had already gone out to the barn to begin milking the cows, and Mom was clearing the table. Finally, she was fed up with my rebellious know-it-all spirit and grabbed me by the arm, turned me over her knee and began to spank me! Well, even though she was just a little thing, her hand was stinging my backside pretty good, but I was determined not to give in. When she finished spanking me, with I'm sure every ounce of energy she had, I stood up, looked her in the eye, and smirked, as if to say – "Is that all?" She was not a bit pleased with my continued rebellion and firmly said, "You go out and see your father!"

Well, as I said, Dad was already in the barn beginning to milk the 50 some dairy cows that we had there on the farm. I didn't really want to face Dad, and so I slowly made my way that one hundred yards or so out to the barn. As quietly as I could, I slipped

[5]Charles R. Swindoll, *The Tale of the Tardy Oxcart*, Nashville, TN, Word Publishing, 1998, pp. 358-359.

through the door on the opposite end of where I knew he would be. As I made my way down the center of that barn, I saw him huddled beside a big old cow assisting her as she finished milking. (I never could figure out as a kid how that in the time it took me to walk from the house to the barn, my dad would find out about what I had done. It dawned on me one night as I was telling this story that the reason my parents had a phone in the house and in the barn was so that my mom could call my dad and tell him all about me before I arrived!)

Dad's back was to me, and I didn't think he had noticed me slipping in. I quietly stood behind him, waiting for him to finish with the cow. (I had been taught as a kid never to disturb my dad when he was working, especially around the cattle. That night, I didn't care if he worked the rest of his life – I was in trouble!) With his back still to me, he pulled the automatic milker off the cow, stood up to release the hoses, picked up the milking machine, stepped over the gutter, and turning around looked into my face. As my eyes met his, the tears were already flowing freely down his cheeks, his lips began to quiver, and he simply said, "John, your sin makes me so sick." For a few brief moments he stood there and wept over my life.

No amount of corporal punishment could have accomplished what those tears did that night. I wished in those moments that my dad would grab me by the neck and throw me against the wall or take a board and beat me – I deserved it! But he never said another word, or did another thing. He just wept in love over my life.

Although my teen years were far from perfect, would you like to know what kept me from going with my friends to the drinking parties after football games? Do you want to know what stopped me from accepting those invitations from the "in-crowd" to drink, take drugs, listen to rock music, go with this girl to that dance, etc.? Oh, I wanted to go, and the temptation was always strong, and sometimes the battle raged in my heart – but I never went, because God would always put that scene of my dad weeping over my sin in front of me, and I couldn't bear the thought of ever going through that again.

Maybe some hot tears from our eyes, fueled by a love in our soul, would help to lead some kids in the right direction today. Remember:

"No one cares how much you know; until they know how much you care."

CHAPTER FIVE

Progress through Perseverance

"Therefore my beloved brethren, be ye stedfast, unmoveable, always abounding in the work of the Lord, forasmuch as ye know that your labour is not in vain in the Lord." I Corinthians 15:58

The ministry of mentoring is not a sprint – it's a marathon. Remember, we are making people, not popcorn. There are no shortcuts to building lives. C. B. Eavey says: "There are no shortcuts to truly Christian leadership. The faith upon which true Christian education is founded is demanding, rigorous, and costly. Christians should be faced with this fact, for never will leaders be produced by lowering standards. Real leadership will come only as Christians follow completely the teachings of God's Word. Nothing will be accomplished through mere dreaming or wishful thinking; what is necessary is entire consecration of Christians to God and such devotion to the task He has given that nothing will be left undone which will contribute to truly effective Christian education."[1]

If God has called us to ministry, then there can be no looking back. "No man, having put his hand to the plough, and looking back, is fit for the kingdom of God." (Luke 9:62) Rest in the promises of God that "faithful is he that calleth you, who also will do it," (I Thessalonians 5:24), and "being confident of this very thing, that he which hath begun a good work in you will perform it until the day of Jesus Christ." (Philippians 1:6)

A veteran missionary once described Eastern European Christians as commitment-rich and information-poor, and Western Christians as information-rich and commitment-poor. Too many of us in the church in the West are slouching into a deformed, under-developed posture because of commitment deficiency.[2] This day of "comfort-zone" living has robbed us of the grit and determination that was woven into the character fabric of our forefathers. The road of ministry is not all interstate – there are some up-hill mountain roads that are only conquered by those with a faith in God and a will to persevere.

William Carey said of his biographer: "If he gives me credit for being a plodder, he will describe me justly. Anything beyond that will be too much. I can plod. I can persevere in any definite pursuit. To this I owe everything."[3]

Calvin Coolidge exhorted: "Press on. Nothing in the world can take the place of persistence. Talent will not; nothing is more common than unsuccessful individuals with talent. Genius will

---

[1] C. B. Eavey, _History of Christian Education_, Chicago, IL, Moody Press, 1964, p. 422.
[2] Howard G. Hendricks, _Teaching to Change Lives_, Portland, OR, Multnomah, 1987, p. 180.
[3] Charles R. Swindoll, _Tale of the Tardy Oxcart_, Nashville, TN, Word Publishing, 1998, p. 438.

not; unrewarded genius is almost a proverb. Education will not; the world is full of educated derelicts. Persistence and determination alone are omnipotent."[4]

Winston Churchill was once asked to give a speech at Harrow School on October 29, 1941. His entire speech was: "Never give in, never give in, never, never, never, never – in nothing, great or small, large or petty – never give in except to convictions of honor and good sense. Never give in."[5]

Perseverance is fueled in the heart. If you are counting on back-slapping, and hand-shaking, and applause to keep you going in the ministry, you won't last long. Our commitment has to be much deeper than that. Ron Lee Davis calls it "intrinsic motivation." Intrinsic motivation is motivation that comes from within. Intrinsic motivation calls forth our innermost resources, values, and beliefs in order to energize our behavior. A Biblical mentor learns to appeal to the intrinsic, inner motivations of the learner, often inspiring behavior that is completely at odds with the extrinsic, outer dynamics of the situation.

This means that the intrinsically motivated person is often inspired to attempt a task precisely because that task is difficult, stressful, painful, and personally costly... When Nehemiah motivated his people to rebuild the wall around Jerusalem, he didn't say, "We're going to make a fun little spare-time project out of this. If the weather gets a little too hot, we'll knock off early. If anybody gets tired, well, there is a lemonade stand and some shade trees over there. Donate an hour, two hours, whatever you can spare. Jerusalem's going to be here a long time, and with your help, we'll get this wall built eventually."

---

[4] Ibid, p. 441.
[5] Ibid, p. 438.

No, Nehemiah gave a tough challenge, a demanding challenge. "You see the distress that we are in," he says. "Come and let us build the wall of Jerusalem, that we may no longer be a reproach." There is urgency and insistence in his call.

Nehemiah motivated his followers in much the same way Winston Churchill intrinsically motivated the people of Great Britain to dedicate themselves to the war effort during the darkest days of World War II. He said, "I have nothing to offer you but blood, sweat, and tears [not a very motivational beginning, is it?]. Victory at all cost, victory instead of terror, victory however long and hard the road may be; for without victory there is no survival. We shall not flag or fail. We shall go on to the end. We shall fight France, we shall fight in the seas and oceans, we shall fight with growing confidence and growing strength in the air; we shall defend our island whatever the cost may be and we shall never surrender. Death and sorrow will be the companions of our journey, hardship our garment, constancy and valor our only shield. We must be united! We must be undaunted! We must never give up![6]

Oh, we need some of that today! We need the "quitters never win, and winners never quit" philosophy in the ministry. Mentoring the next generation is going to take our lifetime – but it's the lifetime of ministry that has the impact. The flash in the pan – the morning glory mentor, has no lasting effect. T. S. Henderson says: "The weakest living creature, by concentrating his powers on a single object, can accomplish something; the strongest, by dispersing his over many, may fail to accomplish anything. The drop, by continual falling, bores its passage

[6] Ron Lee Davis, *Mentoring: The Strategy of the Master*, Nashville, TN, Thomas Nelson, 1991, pp. 140-141.

through the hardest rock; the hasty torrent rushes over it with hideous uproar, and leaves no trace behind."[7]

Let me encourage you to persevere in three vital areas:

Persevere through Fear

Dr. B. Myron Cedarholm was a "preaching machine." He would admonish us: "Always be ready to preach, pray, or die!" It seemed he could preach on any subject at the drop of a hat (and for a long time, too). I recall a young man asking him once, "Dr. Cedarholm, do you still get nervous before you preach?" His answer was classic: "I'd be nervous if I wasn't nervous." One night, I was sitting next to Dr. Paul Levin at the Bill Rice Ranch in Murfreesboro, Tennessee. "Dr. Paul" started in evangelism when he was 15 years old! For over thirty years he had preached at every teen week the Bill Rice Ranch had ever conducted. I suppose he had seen every kind of teenager there was. He seemed particularly nervous that night. He was turning pages in his Bible and scratching out a few last second notes on his sermon outline. During the special music, I lightly tapped him on the knee, and said, "I'll be praying for you tonight, Dr. Paul." I'll never forget what he said. He looked up at me and said, "Thanks, Brother John. You know, people say – trust the Lord – just trust the Lord. I do trust the Lord, but I don't trust the devil! Satan wants these kids tonight – I need God's help."

Moses was afraid. Joshua was afraid. Gideon was afraid. Paul told the Corinthians in I Corinthians 2:3: "And I was with you in weakness, and in fear, and in much trembling." Sounds like your first sermon, doesn't it? Describes your first day of teaching, doesn't it? Reminds you of the first time someone asked you for

---

[7] T. S. Henderson, _The Good Teacher_, Philadelphia, PA, American Baptist Publication Society, (No date printed), p. 118.

advice, doesn't it? The truth is, it ought to describe the last time we preached, or taught a lesson, or gave counsel! Don't run from your fears – let them drive you to the source of your strength and power. Paul goes on to say in that same passage: "And my speech and my preaching was not with enticing words of man's wisdom, but in demonstration of the Spirit and of power: That your faith should not stand in the wisdom of men, but in the power of God" (I Corinthians 2:4-5). "Fear thou not; for I am with thee: be not dismayed; for I am thy God: I will strengthen thee; yea, I will help thee; yea, I will uphold thee with the right hand of my righteousness." (Isaiah 41:10)

Persevere through Failure

I don't know about you, but I find comfort in knowing that Jesus did not succeed with every person to which He ministered. Think about it – Jesus never preached anything less than a perfect sermon, never gave anything less than a perfect object lesson or illustration, never once gave less than perfect advice, for He was perfect in every way. But when He approached the city of Jerusalem, "he wept over it" (Luke 19:41) and lamented in Matthew 23:37, "O Jerusalem, Jerusalem, thou that killest the prophets, and stonest them which are sent unto thee, how often would I have gathered thy children together, even as a hen gathereth her chickens under her wings, and ye would not!" Even one of His own disciples, whom he had personally mentored for three years, betrayed Him!

I wonder how many preachers have succumbed to discouragement over a few critical church members and quit the ministry, all the while dozens of others were growing and maturing under their leadership. I wonder how many teachers have quit their position because of a few trouble-makers, never realizing the impact they were having on the students who were learning. How easy it is to focus on the ones who don't respond. I'm not saying that we shouldn't "weep o'er the erring one" as the song says, but don't quit over him!

Again, I am encouraged by the words of T. S. Henderson: "Our work is not like that of the painter or sculptor: when the painter lays down his pencil, or the sculptor his chisel, and afterwards returns to his canvas or his marble, he finds his work just as forward as he left it. But our addresses are like writing on the sands at an ebb-tide; when we come to continue and finish the writing which we had begun, we find that the tide of worldly feeling and sinful passion has obliterated former impressions, and we have to go over the work again. . . . A Christian mother was known to affirm that she was never weary of repeating a thing, though it were twenty times over, if so in the end she could fix it in her child's mind. It is by dint of perseverance like hers that we must attain our aim. Patience must have its perfect work. Instead of turning aside, appalled at the obstacles which stand in our path, let us learn so to plant our foot upon them, that we may transmute what might have been stumbling-blocks into stepping-stones that shall facilitate progress."[8]

I enrolled in the Maranatha Baptist Bible College in the fall of 1970. B. Myron Cedarholm, the president – mentioned earlier, had been an All-American running back for the University of Minnesota football team in the late 1930's. Although, Maranatha was only in its third year of existence, he was determined to start a football team. Having played in a fair-sized high school with some success, I was more than eager to participate. I'll never forget the day we showed up for practice and were issued our "equipment." It looked like it had been purchased at various garage sales from

---

[8] Ibid, p. 113-114.

moms cleaning out their attics from their son's "Pop Warner" days twenty years before. Helmets without padding, shoulder pads held together with duct tape, and hip pads that came off the ark with Noah! We did get new pants and jerseys, but they were for both practice and games – the only thing that made them look different for game day was the extra bleach we had poured into the washing machines the night before. If we needed tape or arm pads, we had to buy them ourselves. We drove our own cars to away games and played our home games on a high school field two miles from campus. Our locker room had twenty lockers in a room fifteen by fifteen, two metal folding chairs, and four shower stalls, but only two of them produced any water!

We played four games that first year and lost them all. I guess recruiting didn't go too well, because when I returned for my sophomore season, only 18 guys tried out for football! You need 22 just to scrimmage! What a year that was. We played eight games and lost them all. In fact, we never scored! Not one touchdown, not one field goal, not even a safety in eight games. Every week we got beat 40 – 0; 52 – 0; 63 – 0; but the worst came at a home game against Northland College from Ashland, Wisconsin. As we warmed up in the end zone that warm October day, I remember looking up and seeing two greyhound buses and three vans pulling into the parking lot – all with Northland College written on the side. I watched in horror as 90 football players unloaded from those buses and vans. Ninety! We had 18 guys and suddenly most of them were injured!

We went out for the toss of the coin, and I must point out that we won the toss of the coin. It was the only thing we would win all day – but we won the coin toss. They kicked off, but our receiver fumbled the ball, and they recovered near our end zone. On their first offensive play, they ran a dive off-tackle and scored.

They kicked off again, and although we managed to run the ball back without fumbling, on our first offensive play, the ball was intercepted and returned for a touchdown. Within the opening minute of that game, we had fallen behind 14 – 0. And it only got worse. By half-time, nine different Northland players had scored and the scoreboard showed us down 63 – 0. It was only half-time!

As we walked off the field for the half, the Northland coach approached ours and said, "Coach, this is embarrassing. We should not be playing you guys. We have 90 players and they are all scholarship athletes. You only have 18 boys, and someone could get hurt the way this is going. Let's just call it a game. It's already 63 – 0; there's no sense in making this any worse." Well, I was certainly in favor of his proposal. I was never a math wiz but I knew 63 plus 63 was 126 and 0 plus 0 was 0! Our coach however, glared at him, and said, "No, we will finish this game!" I thought he was crazy. I was beat up physically and emotionally and had no desire to play any more football that day.

We played that second half and Northland did their best to ease up on us. The time keepers let the clock run to speed the game up. The final score: 92 – 0! It was a modern-day record. Newspapers all over the nation carried the story. Sports Illustrated had an article about the little Baptist school in Wisconsin that had gotten beat 92 – 0!

I remember sitting on "one" of those metal chairs in the locker room after the game with my head in my hands. I didn't want to see anybody or talk to anybody. I sat there for about an hour until I thought everyone else had left the locker room. When I pulled my hands from off my face, sitting next to me in the "other" metal chair, was my teammate, Randy Peterson. Randy had played in a large Colorado high school program and had offers to play at several big-name schools. He was sitting in the same position as me with his head buried in his hands. I'll never forget our brief conversation – two college football players crying like babies, embarrassed to leave that locker room – we looked at each other and said, "We can't quit! We can't quit! This is too great a game and too much is at stake in our lives to quit! We've got to somehow keep playing and help our teammates to keep going."

It was a long year. Practices were agonizing and games were worse. People laughed at us and joked about our ineptness. But I'm glad we didn't quit. Yes, we lost every game that year, but the following year we won our first game. A boring uneventful 10 – 6 win – but it was a win! Sports Illustrated again carried an article, calling it a miracle! As I think back on it, I believe it was – I think God was embarrassed and had a whole lot more to do with us winning that game than we did.

You know, as I recall the names and faces of those 18 football players on that team, almost to a man, they are faithfully serving the Lord today! Why? Because we learned something through failure, that success could not have taught us. We had learned to persevere!

Persevere through Favor

I like the character of Joseph in the Bible. Certainly, if there is a good example of someone who persevered in spite of some obstacles it was Joseph. But interestingly, Joseph is not only an example of perseverance through difficult circumstances, but he is also a great example of someone who was faithful "in spite of his success!" Take a look sometime at Genesis 39, and count the number of times God refers to this young man as "prosperous" and "having favor." But with all his success, he didn't lower his standards, or give in to the wicked pursuit of an evil woman. He had it made – he was second in command – his brothers had rejected him – there were no other believers around – he didn't need to stay true to his convictions. But he persevered!

How often has success ruined an athlete, a politician, or a business person? And it can ruin us in the ministry too. Don't be sidetracked from your calling to the ministry of mentoring. The stakes are too high and the rewards are too rich to quit for any reason.

I've closed each chapter with a short quotation to encourage you, but here I leave you with a portion of a famous speech by Teddy Roosevelt. I hope it will spur you to "Progress through Perseverance."

It is not the critic who counts; not the man who points out how the strong man stumbled, or whether the doer of deeds could have done better.
The credit belongs to the man who is actually in the arena;
Whose face is marred by dust and sweat and blood; who strives valiantly; who errs and comes up short again and again;
Who knows the great enthusiasms, the great devotions, and spends himself in a worthy cause;
Who, at best knows in the end the triumph of high achievement;
And who at worst, if he fails, at least fails while daring greatly.
It is far better to dare mighty things, to win glorious triumphs, even though checkered by failure, than to rank with those poor spirits who neither enjoy nor suffer much because they live in the gray twilight of life, knowing neither victory nor defeat.

- Theodore Roosevelt

CHAPTER SIX

Enlarging through Envisioning

"And let us consider one another to provoke unto love and to good works." Hebrews 10:24

In the musical *My Fair Lady*, British speech professor Henry Higgins makes a bet with a friend that he can transform a poor Cockney flower girl, Eliza Doolittle, into a refined, blue-blood society lady. To assure his success, the professor not only works with the girl on her manners, speech, and dress; he also spreads the word that he will escort a refined, beautiful princess to London's biggest ball of the year. He knew the power of expectations!

Weeks later, when the door to Higgins's gilded carriage opens, a gasp goes up as the crowds see what they expect to see: a dainty, elegant princess. Throughout the evening, Eliza's speech and actions are profoundly shaped by the city's expectations of her. At one point the professor asks the orchestra conductor his opinion of the "princess."

"I've seen hundreds of balls all through Europe," the wizened old conductor says, "and that one was brought up in the most refined of all palaces."

In the middle of the play Eliza makes a profound statement. She says the real issue isn't how she acts, but what people expect of her. And she says it was Professor Higgins's expectations that caused her to change the most. That is how a girl of the streets becomes a "fair lady."[1]

Expectations are a powerful tool, especially in the ministry of a mentor. Many young people fail today because that's what everyone around them expects – a failure. When children are constantly told, "You can't do anything right" or, "I knew you'd mess that up" or, "You are so stupid," what do we expect them to think of themselves? Remember, they are the followers – we are supposed to be leading them. The product cannot rise above the pattern.

We've got to dream for them! We must see them being a success before they do. As mentors we are trying to facilitate change, growth, and progress, but we have to have an idea of what the finished product is going to look like. Disney World was not completed until after the founder Walt Disney died. When the park opened and was filled with families enjoying the fun, one of the executives said, "It's too bad that Mr. Disney never saw this." Another replied, "He did." Long before any rides were constructed and any tickets were sold, Walt Disney had seen the finished product in his mind.

What do you see in the teenagers of your church? What do you see in that elementary school class? What do you see in your own children? Too often, they never become anything great for God, because we don't expect them to. If you think about it, you are probably where you are right now in your Christian life

---

[1] Bruce Wilkinson, *The Seven Laws of the Learner*, Sisters, OR, Multnomah Press, 1992, pp. 81-82.

because someone believed in you and spent some time trying to encourage you.

In the book *Fathering a Son*, the authors say the following: "The way you treat your child determines how he will feel about himself. Your opinion of him will determine his opinion of himself. As the father, you can give your child the gift of self-esteem. You can help him have a healthy appreciation for himself, a self-confidence that helps him cope with success or failure. If you respect him, trust him, show interest in him, and compliment him, you increase his sense of self-worth. Sarcasm, verbal abuse, and simply not spending time with him destroy his self-esteem and help prepare him for failure.[2]

My high school football coach always had higher expectations for me than I did. I was not the biggest kid on the team, but because of my quickness, I had won a spot on the defensive line. I could get off the ball faster than anyone else and could often get through the offensive line without being blocked. This resulted in a lot of quarter-back sacks and tackles for loss. However, in practice, whenever we would work on that aspect of the game, the coach would make me go through the quickness drills more often than anyone else. He would line everyone else up in lines about four or five players deep, but he would always put me in a line by myself, so that as soon as I would run through the drill once, I would immediately have to go again. Everyone else got to rest for a few minutes between the repetitions, but I had to run that drill continuously. I was pretty upset about this treatment, and so one night after practice I went to the coach and demanded to know why I had to run through that drill more than anyone else. He said, "John, you are the quickest man on our team, but if you keep

---

[2] Paul Heiderbrecht and Jerry Rohrbach, *Fathering a Son*, Chicago, IL, Moody Press, 1979, pp. 29-30.

working hard, you could be the best in the conference." I had reached a plateau of satisfaction in my progress, but the coach expected more.

I recall another similar incident in college. I had not applied myself much in high school or my freshman year in college. I had gotten by with B's and C's and was satisfied with that. In my sophomore year, I was required to take my first year of Greek, and was, needless to say, a little concerned about this class. However, my football coach was the Greek teacher, and so I figured he would go easy on the athletes in the class. To my shock, he cornered two of us after the first class and said, "I believe you two guys could get an A in this class – I dare you to do it!" He turned around and walked out, leaving us to ponder the challenge. That simple statement was all I needed. I began to study like never before and when the semester ended, I had not only received an A in Greek but in all seven of the courses I was taking that semester! Straight A's for the first time in my life – because a teacher/coach expected it!

How can we raise our level of expectations for those we have been given to mentor? How can we "enlarge through envisioning?"

Aim at Being an Exhorter

"He who aims at nothing – hits it every time!" Hebrews 10:24 says: "And let us consider one another to provoke unto love and good works." We are to consider in order to "stir up." Bruce Wilkinson points out that "the Greek word consider means to scrutinize, to evaluate, to constantly look at your audience and ask, 'Where are they? Are they with me right now or not? What are their needs? How can I adjust my content and delivery to teach them more effectively?"[3]

We need some "Barnabas" mentors. The name Barnabas means "Son of Consolation or Exhortation." I like what the Bible says about this man in Acts 11:22-24: "Then tidings of these things came unto the ears of the church which was in Jerusalem: and they sent forth Barnabas, that he should go as far as Antioch. Who, when he came, and had seen the grace of God, was glad, and exhorted them all, that with purpose of heart they would cleave unto the Lord. For he was a good man, and full of the Holy Ghost and of faith: and much people were added unto the Lord." Barnabas was an exhorter and full of faith – full of expectation! In the next verse we find him headed to Tarsus "for to seek Saul." Back in Acts 9:13-14, Ananias was commissioned by God to visit this man Saul, but his response was: "Lord, I have heard by many of this man, how much evil he hath done to thy saints at Jerusalem: And here he hath authority from the chief priests to bind all that call on thy name." Ananias was hesitant, because of Saul's reputation, but notice what the Lord told him in verse 15: "Go thy way: for he is a chosen vessel unto me, to bear my name before the Gentiles, and kings, and the children of Israel." God "expected" great things from this man and now He needed some mentors to catch that same vision of expectation!

Barnabas spent a whole year with Paul mentoring him in Antioch, and the rest is history, as they say. The children in our class, youth group, or home need to be "stirred up" and "exhorted" to love and to good works. God commands us to aim at exhortation: "But exhort one another daily, while it is called To day; lest any of you be hardened through the deceitfulness of sin." (Hebrews 3:13)

---

[3] Wilkinson, p. 77.

William Barclay says: "One of the highest of human duties is the duty of encouragement. It is easy to laugh at men's ideals; it is easy to pour cold water on their enthusiasm; it is easy to discourage others. The world is full of discouragers. We have a Christian duty to encourage one another. Many a time a word of praise or thanks or appreciation or cheer has kept a man on his feet. Blessed is the man who speaks such a word."[3]

"A man hath joy by the answer of his mouth: and a word spoken in due season, how good is it." (Proverbs 15:23)

Affirm as Well as Evaluate

As we "consider" those that we are mentoring, it is easy to see their deficiencies and faults. Our human tendency is to start with those negatives and attempt to correct the problem. A mentoring relationship requires that we be objective and honest, clearly pointing out the areas that are contradictory to the Word of God, in our followers' lives.

But successful mentoring requires both toughness and tenderness. Ron Lee Davis points out that effective mentors "will seek to envision and encourage the possibilities that are latent in the learner's character." He further states, "We will unconditionally accept the learner, even when he fails, and we will encourage him to keep persevering until he reaches his goal."

He then gives the following illustration from a book by Joyce Landorf: "You are the parent of a grade school child, and your child brings home a report card. On that report card are five very good grades and one D. What is the first comment you make about that report card? Do you look at those five good grades first and say, 'Hey, look at those grades! Good job! I'm sure proud of the

---

[3] Charles R. Swindoll, _The Tale of the Tardy Oxcart_, Nashville, TN, Word Publishing, 1998, p. 179.

work you did in those subjects!' And then do you come back later and add, 'Now, let's put our heads together and figure out a way to bring up this grade over here.' If that is your response, then you are an affirmer.

But if your response to that report card is to zip right past those five good grades and hone in on that one low grade; if your first response is to growl, 'What in the world is wrong with you?' then you must admit that you have the tendencies of an evaluator."[4]

We must earn the right to confront through affirmation. If those that we mentor know that we love them, and are on their side, they will be more likely to take our rebuke for those areas that need changing in their life. Our goal is to build up, not tear down. A principle that is vital here is to "affirm in public; correct in private." This assures the young person that you are not trying to destroy them, that you really care how they turn out, and that you are for them.

Jim Burns states: "For every critical comment we receive, it takes nine affirming comments to even out the negative effect in our life." He then goes on to illustrate the power of expectation through affirmation with the following Biblical example: "Jesus had the power to draw out the best in people. He met a clumsy, big-mouthed fisherman named Simon. He looked Simon straight in the eye and said, 'So you are Simon, the son of John?' Simon nodded. Jesus then said, 'You shall be called Cephas' (which in Greek means "the rock"). Most of Peter's friends and family had a good laugh at his nickname. No one would have believed that one day this fisherman would be the leader of the church in Jerusalem. Jesus looked beyond Peter's problems, personality quirks, and sin.

---

[4] Ron Lee Davis, *Mentoring: The Strategy of the Master*, Nashville, TN, Thomas Nelson Publishers, 1991, p. 66.

Jesus saw Peter not only for who he was, but for what he could become. Even three years later after their conversation, when Peter so blatantly denied Jesus, Jesus stood by him and Peter was changed. Simon became what Jesus knew he could become."[5]

Anticipate what you Expect

Wayne Gretzkey, (called "The Great One" in the sport of hockey) was once asked the reason for his success. He said, "I always skated to where the puck was going to be, not to where it had been."

Expectations affect both our attitude as a mentor and our actions. Various research has been undertaken over the years to discover how expectations impact teaching. Here are the findings:

When interacting in class, teachers with low expectations tend to:

> Wait less time for the student to answer a question.
> Call on the student less frequently to answer a question.
> Inappropriately reinforce an incorrect answer of the student.
> Prematurely give the student the answer or call on somebody else.
> Withhold helpful clues and fail to repeat or rephrase the question.
> Give briefer and less informative feedback to the student's questions.
> Interrupt more quickly when the student makes mistakes.

---

[5] Jim Burns, *The Youth Builder*, Eugene, OR, Harvest House Publishers, 1988, p. 54.

When setting the level of achievement, teachers with low expectations tend to:

Criticize the student more often for failure.

Praise the student less often for success.

Write fewer explanatory notes on graded papers.

Teach at a significantly slower and less intense pace.

Fail to give the benefit of the doubt in borderline cases.

Use fewer of the most effective but time-consuming instructional methods.

Assign more busy work than meaningful projects.

When relating personally to the student, teachers with low expectations tend to:

Fail to give specific or positive feedback concerning the student's public response.

Pay less attention to and interact less frequently with the student.

Interact with the student more privately than publicly.

Engage in friendly interaction less often.

Smile less and limit encouraging physical touch.

Maintain eye contact less often.

Limit positive nonverbal communication reflecting attentiveness and responsive-ness, including leaning forward, positive head nodding, and general supportive body language.

These actions clearly demonstrate how students believed to be low achievers often fail to learn adequately or behave appropriately. They are not treated like students who are believed to be good students. Teachers appear to "cause" their students to decline by providing them with fewer educational opportunities and by teaching them less material less skillfully.[6]

If you can't honestly love all of the children in your class or teens in your church, at least love the "potential" that they have. Skate to where the puck is going to be, not where it is now. Proper love for those that God has given us to mentor is described in I Corinthians 13. and in verse 7, it says that love "beareth all things, believeth all things, hopeth all things, endureth all things." Maybe the bearing has to do with where the puck is now, but the believing, and the hoping, and the enduring, has everything to do with love for where the puck is going to be!

What we envision for those following us may have a greater impact on our success than we think. The following illustration makes the point painfully clear!

I stood like a rock in a rushing stream of preoccupied Bible College students. It was fall registration. Organized chaos. I'd seen it all before many times, but this time instead of racing around the gymnasium signing up for classes, I watched as students signed up for my classes. It was my first year out of graduate school, and I was just hours away from my debut on the other side of the lectern.

Taking a closer look at several registration tables, I noticed that I had been assigned sections one, two, and three of the course called "Bible Study Methods." The remaining five sections were taught by others. After walking around for twenty minutes, I left the gym and headed across campus to my office. A well-seasoned faculty member at the college caught up with me and said, "I just can't believe it!"

"You can't believe what?"

---

[6] Wilkinson, pp. 87-88.

"They gave you section two, didn't they?"

"Well, yes, I guess they did."

He shook his head in seeming unbelief. "I just can't believe it. You're the new faculty member – first year rookie – and they gave you section two."

He had me perplexed. "Why – what's so special about section two?"

"You mean they didn't tell you at faculty orientation?"

The truth was, I was the only new faculty member that year, so they didn't have faculty orientation. I asked him to explain it to me.

"Section two has all the top high school seniors coming into the freshman class. The honors group. Cream of the crop. The most outstanding group of students in the whole college."

We stopped outside the faculty offices and he leveled his gaze at me. "Bruce, you are not going to believe the difference teaching section two."

"What do you mean?" I asked, not knowing whether to feel exhilarated or intimidated. Growing up, I had never been in a section two, I didn't think. . . .

"Motivation! Like a team of wild horses straining at the reins. Those kids'll just pull it out of you. You're going to love every minute of it. Wow! First-year teacher. I can't believe the luck."

He walked down the sidewalk, shaking his head. I was intrigued, to say the least.

The next day, section one filed in and we had a good hour. Nothing outstanding, just a good give and take session with a solid group of young men and women.

After break, section two walked in. I couldn't believe it. He was absolutely right. I could feel the electricity in the air. From the ring of the bell, class just flew by as the teacher and students learned at almost warped speed. It was like stepping on a surfboard and riding the crest of the wave the entire hour.

At times the class's interest and desire to learn swept over me with such intensity that I had trouble staying on top of it. Everything seemed different – their questions, their eye contact, their facial expressions, even the way they sat in their chairs. It was incredible. My colleague was right: these students pulled the best right out of you.

Section three came in later that day, and I realized in only a few seconds they were just like section one. Good, but nothing of the caliber of section two.

As the semester progressed, I found myself increasingly grateful to God for leading me into the ministry of teaching. I'd never felt so challenged and fulfilled. And though I enjoyed all of my classes, section two always made my day.

As we neared midterms, I found myself walking to a faculty meeting with the academic dean, Dr. Joseph Wong. "Well, Bruce," he said, "you're at the halfway point of your first year. The honeymoon is over by now. How do you enjoy teaching college?"

"It's absolutely terrific! It's better than I had ever imagined."

He smiled. "That's great to hear. What's your favorite part of teaching?"

Without thinking, I blurted out, "Section two!"

He raised his eyebrows and stopped walking in order to listen more intently, I thought.

"You have section two? Tell me about it."

It was the first chance I had to express my delight and gratitude for the opportunity to teach thirty of the keenest students I had ever encountered. I must have sung their praise for a couple of minutes as I described the amazing difference between them and the rest of my classes.

The dean looked thoughtful as I went on and on about this gifted group of young men and women. When I had finished he said, "I'm glad you're having so much success, Bruce, but I need to tell you something that may surprise you – there is no honors class this year. We canceled it."

My mouth went dry. "Joe," I said, "you've got to be kidding!"

"No, I'm not kidding. Last year we decided it would be better if we spread the top students through all of the classes. We thought it would add a little more spark to each of the sections."

Dizzy with disbelief, I said, "Joe, I'll catch you in a few minutes. I need to go back to my office for a moment."

I raced into my office and dialed the registrar, sure that my colleague was trying to pull something over on this rookie. "Joyce," I said, "I've got section two of the Bible Study Methods, right?"

"That's right, Bruce."

I swallowed hard. "And Joyce, section two contains all the outstanding students – the top freshman, right?"

"Well, no, Bruce. We cancelled that program last year."

Groaning inwardly, I thanked her and hung up the phone. I couldn't seem to come to grips with what was happening. With utmost reluctance, I reached for my grade book and opened it. I compared the grades of sections one and three with section two. The difference was staggering.

I pulled a stack of ungraded papers off my bookshelf. Stacking sections one and three on top of each other, I compared that pile with the stack from section two by itself. Section two had more pages than the other two sections combined!

I went through the papers, one by one, page by page, and the difference was dramatic. The section two students outshone their peers again and again.

That day proved to be one of the most dramatic learning experiences of my life. I've never quite gotten over it. For the first time, I realized that what I believed about my students made an incredible difference in what they learned in my class.[7]

Start envisioning. Dream some dreams for your students, your church members, your teenagers, your children. Believe in them before they do!

"I touch the future; I teach." - Christa McAuliffe (Teacher aboard the ill-fated space shuttle Challenger)

---

[7] Wilkinson, pp. 73-75.

CHAPTER SEVEN

Training through Trials

"But he knoweth the way that I take: when he hath tried me, I shall come forth as gold." Job 23:10

Knute Rockne was a coach and a mentor, the man who built the "Fighting Irish" of Indiana's Notre Dame University into a major power in college football. He pioneered the "platoon system" of substituting offensive and defensive teams during the game, which revolutionized both college and professional football. Under his leadership, Notre Dame won 103 out of 122 games in thirteen seasons, and for five of those seasons was undefeated. A colorful character with a great sense of humor, he was loved and respected by the young men he coached.

One day, a football column with the heading "Old Bearskin" appeared in the school paper. It was the vilest, most insulting piece of sports journalism ever to appear in print on the Notre Dame campus. It berated the team, insulting Rockne himself, as well as many of the team's star players.

The column continued appearing week after week, filled not only with vicious opinions but with inside information. One week, the column berated a star player as lazy and documented how he had lagged through practice. Another column depicted one player as cocky and arrogant and contained exact quotes of bragging statements this young man had made in the locker room. Another column contained a list of the players who had broken training. Another column described the scrapbook full of clippings that one of the players kept and read daily.

Clearly, there was a spy inside the team who was feeding information to "Old Bearskin."

"Coach, we've got to find this guy and fix him!" said Tom, the latest victim of "Old Bearskin," stomping into Rockne's office and waving a copy of the offending column.

"You're telling me!" Rockne raged. "Did you see what this guy wrote about me last week? Why, I've been libeled! I was over there just this morning, demanding to know the identity of this 'Bearskin' rascal, and the editor of the paper refuses to tell me who it is!"

"Well, what are we going to do, coach?"

"The only thing we can do, I guess," said Rockne. "Get out on that gridiron and show everyone in the state that the 'Bearskin' character doesn't know what he's talking about!"

That season, the fall of 1930, the Fighting Irish won every game they played. Sadly, it turned out to be Rockne's last season as a coach. On March 31, 1931, Rockne was killed when an airplane in which he was a passenger crashed into a field in Chase County, Kansas.

After Rockne's death, the editor of the school paper revealed the identity of "Old Bearskin" - Knute Rockne himself. He had used the column to keep his star players from becoming too conceited and impressed by the publicity and adulation they received. Determined to make a liar out of "Old Bearskin," the Fighting Irish were spurred on to achieve one last undefeated season for their coach – their beloved mentor and anonymous tormentor – before his untimely death.[1]

The Chinese ideogram for crisis consists of two characters: one which means "danger," and the other which means "opportunity." Often when trials come into our lives, we see the danger, but fail to recognize the opportunity. We focus on the negative of the situation and often get angry at God. Instead of allowing God to make us better through the trial, we allow Satan to make us bitter. As mentors, we must help others find the opportunity embedded in each crisis that they face.

When trials come, our natural reaction is to think that God has forgotten us or turned his back on us. We often view failure as final, and the trials in our lives become stumbling blocks instead of the stepping stones that God intended them to be. Life is not perfection – it is progression. Our responsibility in the ministry is to create an environment where people can grow in their faith regardless of the situations they find themselves in.

During the early 1980's, when Steven Jobs was running Apple Computers and the company was reaping three-quarters of a billion dollars a year in sales, a reporter asked Jobs, "How does Apple do it?" Job's reply: "We hire really great people and we create an environment where people can make mistakes and grow."[2]

Someone once said, "Problems are opportunities in work clothes." Within each trial there is an opportunity for spiritual maturity and it is our obligation to seize that chance to help the

---

[1] Ron Lee Davis, *Mentoring: The Strategy of the Master*, Nashville, TN, Thomas Nelson Publishing, 1991, pp. 149-150.
[2] Ibid, p. 86.

person grow.   As parents, pastors, and teachers we often do everything that we can to eliminate the problems. We endeavor to make it as easy as possible for young people to do right and serve the Lord. We want them to be happy and enjoy their Christian life. We don't want them to have to learn anything the hard way through the school of hard knocks, so to speak. Thus, we eliminate any potential failures out of fear that it will discourage them.

I have an "open door" policy with the college students that I work with – that is, I let them know constantly that they can come in any time with any need, and I will listen and try to help. As a result, many come with a variety of problems, all of which have usually reached monumental proportions. The more counseling I did in these situations, the more I began to realize that I could solve about eighty percent of these problems myself. If they were encountering problems with a roommate, I could (since I assign their dorm rooms) move them to a different room. If they had financial problems, I could make a phone call to their pastor or parents and see if I could solicit some help for them. If they had a relational problem, I could contact the other person and see if I could iron out the problem, etc. Now, it would not be wrong to do any of these things, I suppose, but it dawned on me one day, that God was allowing these trials in their lives for a reason. He wanted to use these problems to make them stronger. How foolish I would be to remove what God had purposefully placed into their lives in order to make their life easier.

You see, God wants to build some spiritual "muscle" in his children. He desires that we "be strong in the Lord and in the power of his might." (Ephesians 6:10) To illustrate this, I have often said, You could stand with your feet shoulder width apart, clench your hands into a fist, and then bending your arms at the elbow, curl your fists up to your shoulders, and then let them fall back to their original position. Now if you did this exercise 25, or 50, or even 100 times, it really wouldn't do you much good, except to perhaps build a little flexibility in your elbows (Not to mention how dumb you would look in the process). However, if you took a bar and placed some weight on each end of the bar, and grabbed that bar with your hands and repeated the above exercise, guess what? – you would build some muscles in your arms from "curling" the bar 25, or 50, or 100 times. And, the more weight that you place on the bar, the greater the "test" or "burden" becomes, but the potential of building stronger muscles also increases.

Isn't it amazing how we want spiritual muscle, but we don't want to lift any weights? We want to just "go through the motions" of exercise without any burdens, tests, or failures. At the very least, we want just a light burden and for only a short time. But in the Christian life, as it is in weight training, the more weight you put on the bar, and the more repetitions you do, the greater the strength. The muscles are only made stronger as they are tested and torn. Trials and failures are God's way of building spiritual maturity. (By the way, you should never lift weights without a "spotter" – that is, someone to help you get the weight off if you ever get in trouble. Our spotter is none other than the Lord Jesus Christ Himself who will never allow us to "be tempted above that ye are able; but will with the temptation also make a way to escape, that ye may be able to bear it."(I Corinthians 10:13)

God needed a strong preacher on the day of Pentecost to deliver His message. He needed someone He could trust – someone with some spiritual muscle. Muscle that had been tested and torn to failure and built back up again for this occasion when three thousand would turn to Christ in repentance and faith. Who did God choose? – none other than Peter – a man far from perfect – but one who had been "lifting weights" and was making progress.

I like what Stephen Shores observes about Peter: "Could God forgive such a colossal failure? Was Peter even worth the try? Are we? Yes!. . . Peter found himself not only forgiven, but trusted. He learned that failure is not the ultimate. Failure is the unforgivable sin in American culture – so much so that it often paralyzes the individual in a deep-freeze of depression, self-condemnation, and resignation. The Bible, though, is full of the idea that our failures are reversible in their effects. Peter failed utterly, but not ultimately, for God used him as an awesome force in the early Church. Our Father's ability to forgive and restore far outweighs our capacity for failure."[3]

Just as a football coach would not think of taking his team into a game without practice, so our heavenly Father cannot use us without first taking us through some rigors of trial and failure. As a mentor, it is not our job to somehow "fix" the game of life, but rather we must lead our team through the workout of trials so that victory can be experienced. The Apostle Peter gives us some good strategy in I Peter chapter four as we "train others through trials."

"Expect" Trials

"Beloved, think it not strange concerning the fiery trial which is to try you, as though some strange thing happened unto you." (I Peter 4:12) Trials are not any more unusual for a Christian than practice is for the football player. No athlete would be shocked to find out that he has to practice in order to participate in the game. We must help others realize that trials in our lives are not abnormal – they are a part of God's perfect plan. God has no use for tools that have not been tempered in the furnace of fire.

---

[3] Stephen D. Shores, *Discipleship Journal*, Issue 28, 1985, p. 20.

In high school I took a class in machine shop. The teacher was a no-nonsense kind of man who gave explicit instructions and then let us go to work. I decided to make a screwdriver as a project and give it to my Dad for his birthday. I wanted it to be perfect and so painstakingly went through the process of forming out of a block of steel, the handle and blade on the lathe. I shined that steel with a cloth until you could see your face in the handle of that screwdriver. The final process was to place the shaft of the screwdriver into a furnace to temper or harden the steel. I had watched some of my classmates complete this phase and noticed that the fire had turned their projects an ugly black. They had to spend hours re-polishing and rubbing that steel to get the black out, and even then it did not completely disappear. I decided that I did not want my Dad's gift to be ugly, and so I spared my project the fire. I will never forget the day that I handed that screwdriver in to be graded. The teacher took one look at it and plunged it into a huge screw on the leg of his metal desk and began to twist the handle. Within a few seconds my beautiful screwdriver looked more like the screw! It was twisted and bent in every possible direction by the pressure that the teacher had applied. He looked at me, and said, "You have a beautiful screw driver, but it's worthless. You never put it in the fire, did you?" I learned a valuable lesson that day. People don't buy tools to look beautiful in their toolbox. They want tools that are strong and able to be used to solve the tough problems. That means they have to be made of steel that has been hardened by fire.

If we want God to use us – we must expect the fiery trials. "That the trial of your faith, being much more precious than of gold that perisheth, through it be tried with fire, might be found unto praise and honour and glory at the appearing of Jesus Christ." (I Peter 1:7)

Be "Excited" in Trials

Peter goes on to tell us in verse 13: "But rejoice, inasmuch as ye are partakers of Christ's sufferings; that, when his glory shall be revealed, ye may be glad also with exceeding joy." Don't run from the trials – this is our chance to grow and identify with our Savior.

The attitude of the apostles in the early church was not to run and hide whenever the trials came. They relished these opportunities to suffer for Christ as they knew God would use their testimony during these trials to reach others with the Gospel. Acts 5:40-42 gives us this picture. "And to him they agreed: and when they had called the apostles, and beaten them, they commanded that they should not speak in the name of Jesus, and let them go. And they departed from the presence of the council, rejoicing that they were counted worthy to suffer shame for his name. And daily in the temple, and in every house, they ceased not to teach and preach Jesus Christ."

The Apostle Paul recognized that it was through the trials and particularly his "thorn in the flesh" that God manifested His power upon his life. After God refused to remove this trial, He gave Paul the assurance: "My grace is sufficient for thee: for my strength is made perfect in weakness. Most gladly therefore will I rather glory in my infirmities, that the power of Christ may rest upon me. Therefore I take pleasure in infirmities, in reproaches, in necessities, in persecutions, in distresses for Christ's sake: for when I am weak, then am I strong." (II Corinthians 12:9-10)

"Exalt" the Trials

Trials are something that we can thank God for. Peter goes on in I Peter 4:15-16 and says, "But let none of you suffer as a murderer, or as a thief, or as an evildoer, or as a busybody in other men's matters. Yet if any man suffer as a Christian, let him not be ashamed; but let him glorify God on this behalf."

To have complete victory, we must not only accept the trial from God, but thank Him for it as well. Recently, while preaching to teenagers at Camp Joy in Wisconsin, I had the privilege of hearing the testimony of one of the college-age counselors named Paul Lerand. Paul was born with Torrettes Syndrome which causes him to uncontrollably grunt or twitch his body. He had all of us laughing as he told some of his experiences of digging his foot into the ground, or falling down and beating his head against the floor for no apparent reason. I marveled at how freely he spoke of the ridicule he had suffered as a child in school and the hours he would spend crying himself to sleep. Even as he spoke, his body would jerk and his speech was often interrupted by some unplanned sound. But with a joy on his countenance that is rarely seen, he held the audience of teenagers spellbound with his testimony. Paul told how his parents would often comfort him with passages of Scripture that would assure him that God had designed him perfectly according to His plan. He was taught to accept himself for what he was, but it wasn't until his senior year in high school that complete victory came. His family moved to a new city and joined a new church. One day the youth pastor, realizing that Paul was struggling with his trial, shared with him that he was epileptic. He exhorted Paul to not only accept the way God had made him, but thank God for his physical infirmity. Shortly thereafter, he knelt one day and honestly thanked God for this trial in his life. It was then that God began to use his life to help others. I watched him that week minister to dozens of teenagers who came to him with their trials, wanting his prayers and counsel. He had opportunities to minister that none of the rest of us had because he had exalted the trial.

"Evangelize" in Trials

Our passage in I Peter goes on to explain that others are watching us through our trials and are developing an opinion of God based on our reactions. "For the time is come that judgment must begin at the house of God: and if it first begin at us, what shall the end be of them that obey not the gospel of God? And if the righteous scarcely be saved, where shall the ungodly and sinner appear?" (verses 17-18) Often our testimony goes unnoticed by the world until it is put to some test.

One of my favorite professors in college was Dr. Richard Weeks, a little man physically, but a giant spiritually. The energy and joy that he and his wife brought to the ministry was something I had rarely seen up to that time. Some years after I had finished school, news came that Mrs. Weeks had cancer. As her condition weakened and the cancer went into her bones, she was often hospitalized. I tried to arrange my schedule so that I could go by and see her as often as possible. Dr. Weeks had taught us how to make hospital calls in our pastoral classes, and so I was always a little nervous about seeing her and tried to prepare myself as best I could. I would select a passage that would encourage her and practice reading it. I would think about what I could say and how I would pray before leaving so as to always give her hope. But when I would walk into that hospital room, all of my preparation was in vain. Mrs. Weeks would get a big smile on her face and welcome me with a hearty handshake. Then she would ask me how my ministry was doing and rejoice with any positive results I would share. She would then reach for her Bible and open it and begin to read to me a passage of Scripture! And then she would pray! Never would she ask God to meet her needs, but always prayed that God would meet mine. She'd then shake my hand again, and tell me to come back anytime. I would always leave wondering who was ministering to whom?

Toward the end of her life, when her bones were brittle from the cancer, the orderlies were attempting one day to slide her over in the bed in order to change the sheets. As they did, one of her legs snapped. One of the young orderlies was so upset when he heard the leg break that he ran out of the room weeping. Mrs. Weeks however, called for him to return and kindly took the Bible and shared God's simple plan of salvation and led him to Christ.

When Dr. Weeks suffered a series of strokes some years later that eventually claimed his life, he told me one day in the hospital that he had become bitter over these events. But he said, "John, I have asked God to forgive me. I remembered how my wife suffered such intense pain in her death, and kept her testimony for Christ. I want to die like that. I don't want to die bitter at God for these trials. I want to meet my Savior with a good testimony." And by God's grace, he did.

The world notices when the believer's faith is tested by fire. A faith that cannot be tested cannot be trusted.

Be "Earnest" in Trials

Peter closes this chapter by saying: "Wherefore let them that suffer according to the will of God commit the keeping of their souls to him in well doing, as unto a faithful Creator." (I Peter 4:19) The word commit here has a banking connotation indicating a "down payment." God will pay interest on our commitment in trial. We cannot see all of the results now, but they are forthcoming. We may think that God doesn't notice our faithfulness in the trials, but He does. I love Isaiah 49:15-16: "Can a woman forget her sucking child, that she should not have compassion on the son of her womb? Yea, they may forget, yet will I not forget thee. Behold, I have graven thee upon the palms of my hands." God has His own "palm pilot" and He has your faithfulness written on it! Others may forget, but not God. We must earnestly pursue – victory is coming as a result.

We live in a hard time when almost every person we minister to is going through some kind of trial. Young people are not exempt. Broken homes, physical problems, financial pressures, betrayal, hypocrisy, and hurt accompany the lives of many that we mentor today. These, however, are great opportunities for training.

An unusual evergreen is the lodgepole pine that is seen in great numbers in Yellowstone Park. The cones of this pine may hang on the tree for years and years, and even when they fall they do not open. These cones can only be opened when they come in contact with intense heat. But God has a reason for planning them this way. When a forest fire rages throughout the parks and forests all the trees are destroyed. At the same time, however, the heat of the fire opens the cones of the lodgepole pine; and these pines are often the first tree to grow in an area that has been burned by fire.[4]

"Spiritual maturity does not develop in comfortable surroundings."

---

[4] Charles R. Swindoll, *The Tale of the Tardy Oxcart*, Nashville, TN, Word Publishing, 1998, p. 22.

CHAPTER EIGHT

Strengthening Through Service

"If ye know these things, happy are ye if ye do them." John 13:17

The Indian philosopher Mahatma Gandhi chided Christians when he said, "In my judgment the Christian faith does not lend itself to much preaching or talking. It is best propagated by living it and applying it. When will you Christians really crown Jesus Christ as Prince of Peace and proclaim Him through your deeds..."[1]

Christianity can be summed up in "Basin Theology." We can know what is right and yet like Pilate, call for a basin and wash our hands of the responsibility to do anything with the truth we know. Or we can call for a basin as Jesus did, fill it with water, and wash the disciples feet. Which basin we choose is up to us.

Mentoring young people today must involve both preaching and practice, instruction and involvement, explanation and exercise. The two working together will build strong young men and women. The Apostle James reminds us of this truth: "But be

---

[1] Jim Burns, *The Youth Builder*, Eugene, OR, Harvest House Publishers, 1988, p.83.

ye doers of the word, and not hearers only, deceiving your own selves. . . . Therefore to him that knoweth to do good, and doeth it not, to him it is sin." (James 1:22 and James 4:17)

Mark Lamport remarks, "The primary difference between secular and Christian education is the adjectival descriptor 'Christian.' To be 'Christian,' Christian education must: have God's esteem for the human being, sense the task to be a whole-life experience of growth and maturity, and give opportunity for service through experiential action."[2] The whole purpose of the mentoring process is to reproduce servants. II Timothy 2:2 makes this very clear: "And the things that thou hast heard of me among many witnesses, the same commit thou to faithful men, who shall be able to teach others also." This will never happen as long as we view the ministry as a "job" in which we make a living by putting in a certain number of hours.

There are three elements that we must remember if we are going to successfully mentor toward ministry. Getting young people off the bench and into the battle is not going to be easy in a culture with a "couch potato" mentality. Christianity is only one generation from extinction, however, and unless we are able to motivate young people to serve the Lord, our faith is in danger of becoming a fossil.

Exercise is Vital

Years ago on one of the early space shuttles, I read that they took some honey bees up into space. They wanted to see how these bees would do in the atmosphere. They placed them in a container with food, water, and everything that bees need to survive. Once in the atmosphere, the bees soon discovered that

---

[2] Kenneth O. Gangel, *Christian Education: Foundations for the Future*, Chicago, IL, Moody Press, 1991, p. 14.

they did not need their wings to get around in that container. The law of gravity was no longer present and so they could just float from one place to another. Within a few days, every one of those bees had died. Scientists eagerly performed a number of tests on those bees upon their return and their conclusion was that they had died from a lack of exercise!

The same God who created bees with wings to be used, redeems man for the purpose of service. After telling us how we are saved in the previous verses, God explains why He saved us in Ephesians 2:10: "For we are his workmanship, created in Christ Jesus unto good works, which God hath before ordained that we should walk in them." We are not saved by our works, but once saved, we are saved to do God's work. That's why we are here – we are saved to serve!

Christian schools have allowed our young people to live their Christian life in a "greenhouse" and often have no contact with the unsaved world. We do our best as parents to shield our children from the wrong influences and friends. If we are not careful, the church, the Sunday school, the Christian camp, etc., can all fall into the trap of merely ministering to our kids and never develop outreach into a lost and dying world. As a result, young people come to church to be entertained and any challenge to serve is viewed as an invasion of their happiness.

Whatever happened to "There is joy in serving Jesus?" I never met an athlete who was happy sitting on the bench watching his teammates participate. Every athlete yearns and works hard for playing time. We had a young man on our football team in high school named Karl. He was not much of an athlete – in fact, he was horrible. Not once in four years did he ever get into an actual game. I think the coach was afraid he would get injured. But Karl loved football, and the coach knew it. When other guys got cut from the team, the coach kept Karl because of his desire to play. I used to watch Karl take grass and dirt from the field during warm-ups and rub them into his pants. I saw him on the sideline during the game picking at his skin and getting it to bleed and then rubbing the blood into his jersey. When the game would end, you would look at Karl and guess that he had played every down. His jersey was spattered with blood, grass stain covered his knees, and dirt was ground into his uniform. Karl did everything he could to look like he had been in the game.

Something is wrong with our young people when they have no desire to be in the game. Perhaps the reason is in the next element of importance.

Example is Valuable

We dare not merely "talk" about service; we've got to lead the way! Young people can see right through a mentorship that says, "Do as I say, not as I do." It should not shock anyone to discover that we actually do what we preach and teach about.

Several years ago, I was invited to speak at a conference on soul winning. There were a large number of guest speakers, in fact forty-four of us in all. For an entire week, preacher after preacher taught on soul winning and endeavored to motivate the delegates to win the lost to Christ. One afternoon on the schedule there was a time set aside for people at the conference to actually go out soul winning in the city. Buses were lined up to take people to various neighborhoods for an hour of evangelism. But when the time came to depart, only one bus was needed. About fifty of us piled into that old school bus, and as I sat down on a seat with two of my children, a man across the aisle looked at me and said, "I'm surprised to see you on this bus – aren't you one of the speakers?"

I said, "I guess I thought that since I had preached on the subject, I ought to be willing to live it." I don't know what the other preachers were doing that afternoon, but I'm afraid that as a group, we were not being very good examples of service. Perhaps that is why out of the 5,000 who came to hear the preaching on soul winning, only a very small percentage saw any need to practice the matter.

Being an example in service requires time and sacrifice. But if we aren't willing to lead, who is going to follow. The following story illustrates the point quite well.

Like most physicians of great experience, Dr. Evan O'Neil Kane had become preoccupied with a particular facet of medicine. His strong feelings concerned the use of general anesthesia in major surgery. He believed that most major operations could and should be performed under local anesthetic, for, in his opinion, the hazards of a general anesthesia outweighed the risks of the surgery itself.

For example, Kane cited a surgical candidate who had a history of heart trouble. In some cases a surgeon may be reticent to operate, fearing the effects of the anesthesia on the heart of the patient. And some patients with specific anesthesia allergies never awakened. Kane's medical mission was to prove to his colleagues once and for all the viability of local anesthesia. It would take a great deal of convincing.

Many patients were understandably squeamish at the thought of "being awake while it happens." Others feared the possibility of the anesthesia wearing off in the middle of the surgery. To break down these psychological barriers, Kane would have to find a volunteer who was very brave, a candidate for major surgery who would be willing to accept local anesthesia.

In his distinguished thirty-seven years in the medical field, Kane had performed nearly four thousand appendectomies. So this next appendectomy would be routine in every way except one. Dr. Kane's patient would remain awake throughout the surgical procedure under local anesthesia.

The operation was scheduled for a Tuesday morning. The patient was prepped, wheeled into the operating room, and the local anesthesia was administered. Kane began as he had thousands of times before, carefully dissecting superficial tissues and clamping blood vessels on his way in. Locating the appendix, the sixty-year-old surgeon deftly pulled it up, excised it, and bent the stump under. Through it all, the patient experienced only minor discomfort. The operation concluded successfully.

The patient rested well that night. In fact, the following day his recovery was said to have progressed better than most postoperative patients. Two days later, the patient was released from the hospital to recuperate at home. Kane had proved his point. The risks of general anesthesia could be avoided in major operations. The potential of local anesthesia had been fully realized, thanks to the example of an innovative doctor and a very brave volunteer.

This took place in 1921. Dr. Kane and the patient who volunteered had a great deal in common. They were the same man. Dr. Kane, to prove the viability of local anesthesia, had operated on himself.[3]

Excuses are Vain

The late Monroe Parker used to say, "An excuse is nothing more than a lie wrapped in the skin of reason." It's easy to let

---

[3] Charles R. Swindoll, _The Tale of the Tardy Oxcart_, Nashville, TN, Word Publishing, 1998, pp. 515-516.

young people fail today. They can come up with every excuse in the book as to why they can't serve Jesus Christ. As mentors, however, we cannot allow them to hide behind excuses – we must challenge them to spiritual maturity through service. Whether we like it or not, we are competing against the world, the flesh, and the devil himself for these kids. Satan never takes a vacation and he always has something in his arsenal to attract young people away from the harvest fields.

But we must not give up – we must stay on the trail as a mentor and never take no for an answer. No excuses – no alibis!

You've probably never heard of Charlie Beacham, a southern gentleman with a keen mind and a genial personality. Beacham worked for the Ford Motor Company as its eastern regional manager in Chester, Pennsylvania. Beacham was also a mentor to a young Ford salesman named Lido.

Lido was the son of poor Italian immigrant parents. He had been hired to work in fleet sales at the Chester office, and he was struggling in the job. One day, Beacham noticed Lido walking dejectedly through the garage. "Hey, Lido," he said, throwing one arm around the young man's shoulders, "what are you so down about?"

"Mr. Beacham," the salesman replied, "you've got thirteen salesmen selling in thirteen zones, and you're looking at the guy who finished number thirteen in sales this month."

"C'mon, kid!" said Beacham. "Don't let that get you down! Somebody's gotta be last!" He slapped the young man on the back and walked toward his car. As he opened the car door, he turned and called out to Lido, "But listen! Just don't you be last two months in a row, hear?"

As a mentor, Charlie Beacham was tough but fair. He gave young Lido advice, showed him the ropes of the business, and most important, instructed him in the kind of character needed for success in business and in life.

"Always remember," Beacham once told him, "everyone makes mistakes. Trouble is, most people won't own up to their mistakes. Some guys blame their mistakes on the weather, on their wives, on their kids, on their dogs – never on themselves. If you foul up around here, I want you to come to me and own up to it, no excuses, no alibis."

Charlie Beacham gradually gave Lido more and more responsibility. He assigned him to teach local dealers how to sell trucks. He let the young man produce a sales handbook for the company. He sent Lido on sales and training trips up and down the eastern seaboard.

Lido didn't just learn about the car business from Charlie Beacham. He learned about life, about perseverance, about decision-making, about personal responsibility. Charlie Beacham, Lido later recalled, had "more impact on my life than any person other than my father. . . . He was a great motivator – the kind of guy you'd charge up the hill for, even though you knew very well you could get killed in the process. He had the rare gift of being tough and generous at the same time. . . . He was not only my mentor, he was more than that. He was my tormentor. But, I love him!" Lido took the knowledge, skills, character, and maturity he acquired under the mentorship of Charlie Beacham and put it to good use throughout his career at Ford, and later at the Chrysler Corporation.

The ultimate test of his skill and character came in the early 1980's when, as Chrysler's chief executive officer, he led the company from the brink of disaster ($4.75 billion in debt in 1980) to stratospheric heights of success ($925 million in the black in 1983). Today, as you've already guessed, Lido is better known as

Lee Iacocca. Auto industry analysts attribute the amazing turnaround of the Chrysler Corporation to this one man.

Iacocca, in turn, gives much of the credit for the shaping of his own values and character to his mentor, Charlie Beacham.[4]

Do you remember how Simon Peter in John 21:3 was so discouraged, so fed up with the ministry, that he said, "I go a fishing." Yes, the whole thing had finally caught up with Peter, and apparently the other disciples as well, for they said, "We also go with thee." Ministry had lost its appeal – the honeymoon was over! Someone else can serve – they were going back to making money. But the chapter reveals that as they labored through the night, they caught nothing. And who should show up in the morning on the shore but Jesus Himself. You see, the Master Mentor was not about to give up on these men and especially Peter. The early first-century church was going to need him, and Jesus wasn't about to let the excuses of Satan rob him of the joy of service.

After Jesus had performed a great miracle (153 fish in one cast), had cooked them a meal, He got down to business with Peter. Three times he tested his love with the same question. Each time, as Peter answered in the affirmative, Jesus challenged him with "service" – "Feed my sheep." No more excuses, Peter. No more alibis. There is work to do, and I need you to do it!

Although Peter still made his share of mistakes without a doubt, from this point on, he never looked back. He had heard the call of God, had tasted the joy of serving, and once he put his hand to the plough, there was no going back! What if Jesus had not pursued him that night? What if He had let him go in his

---

[4] Ron Lee Davis, *Mentoring: The Strategy of the Master*, Nashville, TN, Thomas Nelson Publishers, 1991, pp. 135-137.

discouragement back to the world? The real question is, what will happen if we don't engage our young people today in service?

It's going to take time, and planning, and energy to take our young people soul winning. We'll have to work at getting them to take part in a service at the local rest home or prison. Funds will need to be raised to organize and conduct a missions trip. Sure, they'll make some mistakes as we allow them to help in the junior church services and vacation Bible school. But young people will suffer spiritual atrophy unless we get them involved in service. We must "strengthen through service."

"Your job is not to fatten geese, but to train athletes."

Part II

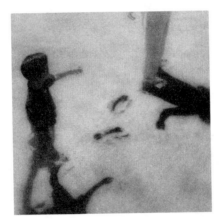

By Dr. Mark Rasmussen

CHAPTER NINE

Energizing Through Experiences

"Those things, which ye have both learned, and received, and heard, and seen in me, do: and the God of peace will be with you." Philippians 4:9

The old saying goes, "History is not boring...it's the teachers that are boring." Unfortunately, that is also true about English, Bible, or you-fill-in-the-blank teachers. Why is it that lectures are often wooden and devoid of even the minutest vestiges of emotion and life? Oft times it is solely because we fail to use energizing experiences from our own lives or the lives of others.

For many years, *American Heritage Magazine* has included a segment entitled "My Brush with History." This article is always a first person account of someone whose life has intersected, albeit often briefly, with some important figure of their generation. The recollections are sometimes humorous, often poignant, and always effective in giving a new understanding of a historical period.

Charles Spurgeon stated over a century ago that illustrations are the windows that allow the light to shine on the truth. It is still true today. Whether from the pulpit, classroom, or in the home, illustrations from our own lives and the lives of others that leave indelible images often teach valuable lessons.

Personal Illustrations

People learn best from people. Notice the method of the Master Teacher as He used parables to illustrate truths and principles.

A segment of history that has fascinated people for generations is the 1920's (see Frederick Lewis Allen's *Only Yesterday* and *Since Yesterday*). One of the pivotal characters of this period was the famous Chicago Bootlegger, Al Capone. Note two different ways that this key figure could be covered.

1) Al Capone was a bootlegger in Chicago. He was eventually captured on income tax charges. He had lived a sinful life and died of syphilis in Miami, Florida.

2) Al Capone was a flamboyant figure, who mocked both God's laws (Proverbs 20:1) and man's laws. He thought that Chicago was "his" city. He used violence and corruption to achieve his goals. A few years ago, journalist Geraldo Rivera announced to the world that there was a secret vault beneath the hotel where Capone had once lived.

Upon hearing this, I asked my wife to go out with me on a date in Chicago. I told her I had to make one little stop first. We made our way to the condemned hotel on Michigan Avenue, where Capone had once lived. The television trucks were already grouped around the abandoned building. My wife and I tried to make our way in but were rebuffed. But there had to be another way! Now deserted by my wife, who had retreated to our vehicle with clear explanation of how to bail me out of a possible incarcerating experience, I made my way to the fire escape.

Up I went to the third floor. Making my way in through a broken window, I maneuvered through the detritus left in the hallway. The hotel had obviously become a home to derelicts, alcoholics, and drug addicts.

At the end of the hallway stood the suite of rooms that had once been occupied by the Capone gang. The area had been swept out and looked as if it were almost ready for occupation. Pictures were taken from several vantage points and a piece of tile was pried from above the sink. Suddenly my heart accelerated and adrenalin flooded my system as the large Chicago policeman entered the room. After being ushered out of the hotel and asked not to return, I quickly made my way back to my waiting wife. Class, how many of you would like to see the tile that I pried off the wall? (Tile begins to make its way around the class).

As for the "rest of the story," the vault proved to be empty of any long lasting valuable and the hotel was demolished a few days later.

Mr. Capone eventually fell and was to lose his fortune, his place of prominence, his health, and even his sanity. The last days of his life found him a babbling idiot, his brain eaten away by syphilis, sitting with a fishing pole line dropped into his swimming pool. He had been released from prison to go home and die.

While both the first and second definitions are totally true, the second will do far more to hold the students interest and to allow for the "teachable moment."

You might immediately tend to think, B*ut that didn't happen to me.* But wait, it did happen to someone you know of...and that is the beauty of sharing energizing experiences – they tend to add life and energy to a truth.

Another area of personal illustrations comes directly from "life lessons." It is imperative that the speaker, whether pastor, parent, teacher or friend, share things that made a difference in his life. Bob Jones Sr. talked about the "dominating truth" that affected every area of his life. Dr. Jones said that as a young man he realized that everyone had to be somewhere forever. This led to an evangelistic and educational ministry that has affected countless lives. From this, I am reminded of the value of a soul.

As a young man, I heard how my father received Christ while in college and how he felt called to the ministry. He recounted how his father told him, "If you go to that school, don't bother to come back home." Fortunately, my father did obey God's call and went on to now what is more than four decades in ministry. From this I saw a testimony of one who chose to obey God rather than man. Years later, his experiences came to mind when I was faced with major career decisions.

Life can oft be boiled down to the essence of the choices that we have made. Many times the correct and incorrect choices that we make have made definite differences in the direction our lives have taken. These truths that we have learned are invaluable aids that must be passed on to other generations.

Unfortunately, people often repeat the old adage, "Experience is the best teacher." While it is true that experience is an effective teacher, it is not always the best teacher. How much better to allow the listener to learn from the experience of others. While I was still a young boy, my father drove several of us boys down to the Sunset Strip in Los Angeles. This was home to many alcoholics. He showed us men asleep on the street covered with accumulated filth and grime. Others laid in the gutter of the street itself. We saw men leaving liquor stores with cheap bottles of fortified wine clutched to their chest as if it was an artifact of great value. Unquestionably, that experience is one of the reasons I have never tasted alcohol after four plus decades.

Obviously, soul-winning illustrations that come from our lives (especially if recent) can serve to kindle a fire in the heart of another believer. The Word of God encourages us to "provoke one another unto love and to good works." (Hebrews 10:24) Our words and lives alike can be used by the Lord to make a difference in the lives of others. There is an overriding responsibility to encourage and help others to be the Christian that God saved us to be.

Historical Illustrations

In restaurant vernacular, it is often stated that you sell the "sizzle" and not the steak. After well over twenty years of classroom experience, I can attest to the fact that both the "sizzle" and the "steak" are of great importance. The statement must precede this segment that pure academics are important. We need to be concerned with finishing the material and even the textbook if at all possible. Content does matter.

The obverse side of the academic coin is related to palatability. It is unfortunate that many teachers tend to take the attitude of "Just the facts, Man, just the facts." Facts, statistics, and details are all important, but it is tantamount that the presentation be as palatable, interesting, lively, and memorable as possible. A re-reading of the parables will enforce the fact that they were interesting!

As the reader, you choose between A and B as to which way would best help you to learn about these isolated facts.

I. *Horrors of Trench Warfare in WW I*

A. Trench warfare was horrible during the first World War. It was dirty, dangerous, and boring. Often, soldiers would be trapped in the same trench for months on end.

B. (to be added to material given above) Some of the problems that were rampant in the trenches are rather nauseating for us to think of today. The latrine facilities often consisted of a trench dug in the middle of the floor, where all slop and human waste were dumped. Because of the ferocity of the artillery bombardments, it was often impossible to get out of the trenches to bury waste or even human remains.

An answer to this dilemma seemed to be to tunnel into the wall of the trench. Unfortunately, this led to an incredible profusion of trench rats that suddenly had an unending supply of easy-to-access food. Rats, which can reproduce in just 21 days, soon became a scourge to the military. Rats' teeth never stop growing, and soon many a soldier began to dream of lost appendages.

II. *The Creation of the Food and Drug Administration (FDA)*

A. Food processing was not always as clean and sanitary as it should have been. The U.S. government began a process of inspecting all meat.

B. Have you ever wondered about the little blue stamp that you often see on meat purchased at a supermarket? If so, you will undoubtedly be interested here in the States. First of all, let me reassure you, that the ink in the stamp that is on your meat is totally edible. The ink that is used is made from the skin of grapes. So you don't have to trim it off ever again.

About 100 years ago, a group of journalists called "muckrakers" (a term interestingly enough taken from Bunyan's *Pilgrim's Progress*) began to investigate and publish reports on various aspects of American life. An area that was of wide interest to many readers was food. One of the muckrakers, Upton Sinclair, wrote a book about the meat industry called *The Jungle.* This book detailed reports of piles of meat in the slaughterhouses that were so covered by rat droppings that the workers had to sweep the meat off prior to its being packaged.

More stories included tales of meat that was green and slimy with spoilage being ground up and heavily spiced for sausage. Others heard stories, some proven, and others no doubt apocryphal, of entire fingers with nail still attached (as if that made it more palatable) being found neatly encased in a sausage link, discovery usually coming upon first bite.

Eventually, the government stepped in and now all meat products are inspected. Let me add, lest you feel too comfortable or complacent, it will probably not encourage you to know that fish will be approved if no more than fifteen percent of the total meat shows any sign of spoilage. *(The total time to tell this is just over a minute.)*

III. *The Commanding Generals of the Revolutionary War*

A. During the Revolutionary War, America had a real advantage when comparing George Washington to men like Gage, Clinton, or Howe. Washington was saved, but the others had problems.

B. Character often makes all the difference, and never was this any more obvious than in the leadership of the combatants during the Revolutionary War. On the American side was Washington, a man memorialized by his praying in the snow at Valley Forge. Compassion, strength, courage, and heart combined to form a true leader of men. Washington was willing to give up his salary for the duration of the war and was adamant that his soldiers not steal from the general populace no matter how dire the shirts they found themselves in.

On the other hand, the British leadership, which had all the appearances of professional soldiery complete with flashy uniforms and the requisite military training, combined their efforts into a true comedy of errors. The mistakes made by the British will undoubtedly be studied at war colleges for centuries. Whether it was Gage's refusal to ever order a frontal attack after the Carnage at Breeds Hill or Howe's decided lack of enthusiasm to go far from Boston (due in large part to his enthusiasm for Mrs. Joshua Loving), choice after choice doomed the British. Finally, Clinton (much like an American politician with the same name) was obsessed with the public's perception of his every decision. He endeavored to keep every piece of paper that ever entered his life ranging from battle musings to laundry lists until cases were being transported from battle site to battle site.

IV. *Jonah goes to Nineveh*

A. Jonah was a prophet who was commanded by God to go to Nineveh. He disobeyed and judgment followed.

B. Have you ever contemplated as to why it was that Jonah wanted to go as far as possible from the place God commanded him to go? Possibly, it was due to the fact that the Ninevite kingdom was known to have a penchant for atrocious tortures that could put fear into the heart of the most stalwart warrior. One historian recounted how that the Ninevites would sometimes choose to kill a victim with the torso covered. Then horizontal lines were cut across the pelvic area and the chest area with a bisecting line cut from sternum to navel. The victim would then have the skin pulled back like the opening to the top of a box. Often, grain or feed would be scattered across this gory opening and ravenous beasts would be allowed to root for food. Now perhaps we can better understand Jonah's reluctance to go to a nation that was definitely not abiding by the Geneva awards.

V. *The Digestive System*

A. The digestive system is the God-created process by which nutrients are extracted from food and put to use by the body.

B. Have you ever wondered exactly how we began to understand the intricacies of the digestive system? Although dissections had been going on for hundreds of years, it was not until an accident occurred in frontier America that doctors really began to understand how the digestive system worked. It all started when a gun was dropped on its butt in front of an old western store. The giant hunting rifle discharged its load and shot a young man right across the abdomen. The damage was horrific. There was nothing to stitch because the exterior abdominal flesh was absolutely destroyed. In fact, the stomach organ was perforated and open to both ingress and egress. A doctor, thinking that his patient had only a few hours to live - at the most, a day or two - was overcome by curiosity. He made use of access to the open stomach by tying bits of meat on a string and dropping them into the stomach. He would then draw them out periodically and record the effect of the digestive system on the meat or other foods. If you are interested in the entire event, please see *The Window of the Stomach.*

After reading these illustrations, certainly at least two truths should be evident. First, illustrations can help to make a long ago event seem both relevant and much more immediate. This is due to the fact that illustrations often find the listener putting him or herself in the middle of the event. They begin to "see" the situation. Of course, it has been said numerous times that "seeing is believing."

Secondly, the illustrations help the students to ask questions. It has often been reiterated by many a teacher that the active mind is a questioning mind.

Although not every single point can be illustrated with a one or two minute illustration, it is crucial to understand that we truly can energize our readers and listeners through the recounting of interesting experiences of the past.

Illustration Sources

A common misconception among those who seek to communicate is that anecdotes and illustrations can only come from a book that has illustrations in the title. Often, the very best sources for illustrations are those that come from daily reading. It was Wesley who said to a nephew who was also a preacher:

> What has exceedingly hurt you in time past, nay, and I fear to this day, is want of reading. I scarce ever knew a preacher read so little. And perhaps by neglecting it you have lost the taste for it. Hence your talent in preaching does not increase. It is just the same as it was seven years ago. It is lively, but not deep; there is little variety; there is no compass of thought; Reading only can supply this, with meditation and daily prayer. You wrong yourself greatly by omitting this. You can never be a deep preacher without it any more than a thorough Christian. O begin! Fix some part of every day for private exercises. You may acquire the taste which you have not; what is tedious at first will afterwards be pleasant. Whether you like it or not, read and pray daily. It is for your life; there is no other way; else you will be a trifler all your days, and a petty, superficial preacher.
> - from THE MESSAGE OF THE WESLEYS,
> edited by Philip S. Watson: a Macmillan Paperback

It seems like it would be virtually impossible to excel as a communicator, whether as a parent, youth leader or pastor, without continual refurbishment of our mental will. The great enemy of the speaker is the constant reiteration of S.O.S. – Same Old Stuff! It must be remembered that if it sounds in the least bit tired, trite, or worn to us, that will undoubtedly be communicated to the listener. Conversely, many times we have heard people communicate something they had just seen or read with excitement and vivacity. This is because it was new and alive to them, and so it was to the listener.

When reading from sources, one of the best places to look is in the daily newspaper. Recent events share both immediacy and credibility. When clipping a source from a magazine or newspaper, always jot the date and the source at the top.

Some years ago, I read that Billy Graham would send an advance team into the city he was to preach in. One of the men would be responsible for looking for local events during the previous few days that could be incorporated into Dr. Graham's sermons. This is one of the things that would make his campaigns seem so applicable to a specific city.

Beyond the newspaper, I have found the best source of illustrative material to be found in a variety of magazine sources. Some of the magazines that we have received for years include *The Smithsonian, Reader's Digest, Newsweek, Saturday Evening Post, American Heritage, Better Homes and Gardens, O Timothy, Biblical Archeology*, and, of course, *Sports Illustrated.*

This is just a starter list and obviously shows the bias of my personal interests. *Smithsonian* and *Reader's Digest* are especially good "general knowledge" magazines and will often serve as starters to pique your interests to a greater degree. I have found with the increasingly greater demands on our time that I find fruit more quickly and regularly via this tool.

Charles Tremendous Jones said years ago that "leaders are readers." That is truer today than ever before. I believe you will be the same person five years from now as you are today except for the books you read, the people you are around, and the things you watch and listen to.

The Apostle Paul asked for his cloak, books, and parchments. If he needed books, we certainly do also. The two greatest objections given to reading are cost and time. If we are to find energizing illustrations we cannot be dissuaded by such easily conquered obstacles. When it comes to cost, think of bargain bins, used bookstores, and especially thrift stores. Beyond that, there are library sales and numerous magazines of closeout book dealers that will often offer pages of books for less than four dollars each. There are numerous sellers of used Christian books that will allow you to build a library affordably. Three that I have found useful are **Cornerstone Books** (P.O. Box 28224, Santa Ana, CA 92799), **Edward R. Hamilton** (Falls Village, CT 06031-5000), and **Publisher's Central Bureau**.

Then comes the problem of time. Like other necessary time consumers such as witnessing, exercise, or family activity, the only way to be successful on a long-term basis is to have a definite time for a definite activity. Start with thirty minutes a day. Undoubtedly, the greatest enemy of reading, writing, and meditation is the omnipresent television and video player. Important decisions have to be made regarding what really holds value for a family. This chapter is not devoted to the media, but suffice to say they hold a pragmatic, humanistic agenda that is the antithesis to all that the Christian should believe. While there are many fine educational programs on the History Channel, Discovery Channel, etc., we must remind ourselves of the necessity of redeeming the time. We may watch an actual surgery take place and be in awe of the intricacies and skill involved, but how useful will that be in the long run.

Filing and Categorizing of Illustrations

Rule number one can be taken from an early Patch the Pirate recording, "Do it now, don't delay, and don't put it off 'til another day." Countless times, the perfect illustration or story was lost because it was not categorized or filed. When a useful illustration is found, immediately photocopy or clip and put it where it will be noticed and used. Illustration notebooks are good, but it is much better to place the illustration or article with a particular lesson or sermon.

General files done topically are also very helpful. Growing up, my term papers tended toward subjects like drug abuse, alcoholism, or rock music. This was due to the fact that my father had been collecting sermon material on these subjects for decades.

When a good illustration is heard, write it down. We should not allow an effective truth to go weakly promoted because we have lacked the true diligence necessary to convey it.

Whether a parent, teacher, youth worker, or pastor, we need to collect just the right experiences and illustrations in order to adorn the truths with a brilliance that will make them palatable and understood by those that God allows us to impact.

CHAPTER TEN
Feeling In Facts

"For precept must be upon precept... line upon line... here a little, and there a little:" Isaiah 28:10

It was during the pre-school years that it all began. Our parents wanted us to memorize certain "very important" numbers. These usually started with our addresses and phone numbers. Since that time, we have been plagued with a myriad of names, numbers, facts, proverbs, sound-bites, and various esoteric that people have convinced us we must remember. We have been threatened that if something is forgotten, a fate worse than death will undoubtedly befall us.

In reality, rote memory truly is important. But it need not be drudgery or torment on us as a medieval inquisition torture chamber. Memory work is a discipline and has long been a linchpin of an educated person, at least until the last fifty years. If memory work were more than a tedious requisition of academia, it would be wise to answer these crucial questions about memorized material. Why should young people memorize? What should young people memorize?　And how should young people memorize?

Why Memorize

The human thought process has been shown to work on an association mode or level.　It is apparent to a young parent that knowledge invariably goes from the known to the unknown.　In the classic work, *The Dictionary of Cultural Literacy*, edited by Jacques Barzun, the implication is made that educated people have a basic understanding of general knowledge in a variety of areas.　These areas include subjects as wide-ranging as mythology, Christianity, world history, American history, sports, literature, etc.　Interestingly enough, these men have broken this material down into gradations ranging from first grade through twelfth grade, as well as the adult manual.　Although I believe entire sections could be skipped over and other sections could receive either less or more emphasis based on my Christo-centric approach or world view, there is no doubt that this basic concept is correct.　People need to know certain foundational facts to function at any level above the marginal.

Young people will learn new truths, facts, and concepts in a way that closely approximates the building of a house.　Hence, the foundation, the family, and other basics must be right or the ultimate "house" will be skewed with walls that are out of square and windows that won't shut.　This could be illustrated by the little girl who grew up in the dairy country of Wisconsin, where the cows far outnumbered the human inhabitants.　Growing up on a large dairy farm where the black and white Holsteins seemed omnipresent and the obvious source of her family's sustenance came from the cow, she came to respect the importance of cows to her family.　One day while making an infrequent visit to the big city, she saw a large woman in a black and white habit laboriously making her way down the street. Leaning out the window she yelled at the top of her voice, "Mommy, look at the cow walking on two legs." She had made an assumption based on previously learned material. While that story may afflict a minor chuckle, it illustrates a truth rather than a truism. The human mind is constantly making myriad associations and assumptions based on previously learned information.

Another core reason that answers the "why?" is that our decisions are only as good as the information upon which we base them. That is why the founding fathers thought it wise to post the Ten Commandments in courtrooms across the land. It was a good idea then and incidentally, it still is, despite the rabid opposition of the ACLU.

This is the reason that Christian parents of the youngest toddler feel an almost immediate need to teach them verses like Ephesians 6:1, "Children obey your parents..." I have no doubt that this was one of the first truths from God's Word that my children were privileged to hear. Our choice of Scriptures is sometimes selective. After catching a child in a lie, we love to point out that Revelation 21:8 says that "all liars, shall have their part in the lake which burneth with fire and brimstone: which is the second death." And when fraternal warfare is in full bloom, we love to quote the passage on "blessed are the peacemakers" with a solemnity appropriate to one who has personally won a Nobel Peace Prize. In reality, this is the use of *"sound words."* We need to realize that it is the Word of God that will not return void. It is important for parents, teachers, and youth workers to choose topical verses that can help to guide their children in the crucial decision-making processes that will ultimately decide the warp and woof of their character.

If Christian young people will truly understand what it means to "honor thy father and thy mother," this will bring forth behavioral decisions that will ultimately stand them in good stead both during their growing up years and ultimately when they stand before the Judgment Seat of Christ. This is the primary reason that necessitates the memorization of Bible truths and principles that are often called "moral values." Those in authority need to understand why the Caesars and Pharaohs insisted on being priest-kings. Words carry a great deal more weight when one can say, "Thus saith the Lord" instead of just saying, "Because I said so."

What Should Young People Memorize?

There are many things that are worthy of memorization. Great speeches, poetry, plays, proverbs, maxims, and principles are all worthy, but only the Scripture is "pure." (Psalm 12:6) Therefore, parents, teachers, and youth workers must all remember that it is God's Word hidden in our heart that will keep us from sin. (Psalm 119:11) Furthermore, the Psalmist states that we can cleanse our way by taking heed to the Word of God.

In American colonial history, young people were taught the sounds of the alphabet by associating a letter with a verse. Therefore, they would learn *A* is All have sinned, *B* is Be ye kind, *C* is Come unto me; instead of *A* is for apple, *B* is for ball and *C* is for cat. God's truth was ingrained into their memory as early as possible.

The use of God's Word truly gives authority to the parent, teacher, and youth worker. Undoubtedly, today's young people are being molded by the videos and music videos that are being watched again and again. The popularity of a given music video is determined by the amount of times it is shown and re-shown on television. The actions that are seen ultimately become learned behavior, and often this is copied to the detriment of society.

The Christian young person needs to have the repetitive force of God's Word continually at work on his life. It is God's Word alone that "pierces even to the dividing asunder of soul and spirit..." For decades, Dr. Charles Homsher and his Neighborhood Bible Time evangelists have based a summer Bible school program on the foundation of Scripture memory. I have no doubt that the time spent, effort expended, and ribbons received for learning God's Word were far more important than an additional ten or fifteen minutes spent making a piece of "original artwork" out of Styrofoam egg cartons.

Unfortunately, it seems as if today's eighteen-year old is more Biblically illiterate than ever before. Our college has a blend of almost one-third home-schooled young people, one-third Christian school graduates, and one-third public school graduates. Dropping from this equation those who were recently saved, we find that across the entire spectrum there is a tremendous need to help young people with general Biblical literacy. This is due in large part to the fact that where we sow an emphasis, we will undoubtedly reap a harvest. One author stated that the average Christian teenager watches over twenty hours of television a week. That could be called sowing an emphasis. In another spectrum, many Christian schools have become so sports-centered that everything else suffers to its exclusion. Things like teen soul winning, academics, and a person's Christian walk often take a back seat to athletics (By the way, sports have an important place in the Christian realm. The key is that they have a place and are not the realm, Luke 2:52). If one really believes that bodily exercise profits little (I Timothy 4:8), and that we are to seek first the kingdom of God (Matthew 6:33), then it stands to reason that

111

every young person could learn at least one verse a week from age four until graduation at age twenty-two. If proper review principles were instituted, and if there were a tri-lateral teamwork with home, church, and school; the *average* young person would have memorized (hid in his heart) a minimum of 936 verses. This would be a bare minimum if any effort at all were expended. A good place to start would be the Ten Commandments, the Roman's Road, and the first and twenty-third chapters of Psalms.

Beyond the diamonds of Scripture, there are many semi-precious stones that would be advantageous for young people to hide away in the jewel box of their mind. As one who has taught college history for over two decades, I realize the temptation that teachers often have to make the students "learn everything." Oft times, we are far better off to show students where or how to find a date than to make them memorize every date which "might" be pertinent to a certain course of study. Obviously, a student should realize that Elizabethan England was not during the 1950-2000 year period, even though Queen Elizabeth II *was* the monarch.

A proper contention might be that memorizing the Presidents of the United States but not the dates of their inauguration and exit would be sufficient. Yes, it would be important to know Presidents who have identical last names and to be able to differentiate between John Adams and John Quincy Adams, etc. Unfortunately, teachers often go into overkill. It is good to know the Tudor dynasty lasted from 1485-1603 and who its monarchs were, but is it really that important to know the ascension date of Bloody Mary? Guy Doud, a former Teacher of the Year, illustrated this well when he mentioned that one of his teachers wanted him to know the names of the Greek gods and goddesses. To top it off, she wanted him to know their Norwegian names also. (Everyone who works with young people should listen to the cassette or watch the video entitled *Teacher of the Year,* available from Focus on the Family.)

In designating facts as memory-worthy, we can decide if they are truly crucial as memory pegs, as turning points, as starting or finishing dates, or if they are arcane facts that will be forgotten seconds after the next test. It is undoubtedly important to know that the Civil War ran from 1861-1865 and that the turning point battle was Gettysburg in July of 1863, but does it really become a matter of life and death importance to know the dates of the Battle of Spotsylvania Courthouse? I, for one, think not.

There are some facts that are necessary for a well-rounded education. Despite computers and calculators, it is still important to know multiplication tables. The parts of speech need to be memorized and understood for lifetime literacy and, of course, those who work with young people will have personal insights as to that which will still matter in later years.

Down through the decades, Christian leaders have become connected with statements like "Three to thrive" and "Everything rises and falls on leadership" by Dr. Lee Roberson, or Dr. Bob Jones Sr., who challenged several generations of college students to "do right." Our own pastor, Dr. Paul Chappell, has exhorted the Lancaster Baptist Church to "keep the main thing the main thing, and the main thing is soul winning." These different leaders reiterated certain truths until they became fixed in the minds of the listeners. Those of us who work with young people should certainly learn from this. It should be carefully thought out as to what we want to accentuate and then the hammer of repetition will forge an understanding in the minds of the hearers. Truths like those found in the little booklet of Dr. Bob Jones Sr.'s chapel sayings are worthy of repetition in homes, classrooms, and youth groups.

It should also be pointed out that required memory work at all age levels is an excellent discipline and a tremendous teaching tool. Speech contests, which require perfect memorization of classic speeches ranging from the *Gettysburg Address* and Macarthur's *Farewell Address* to Jonathan Edwards' *Sinners in the Hands of an Angry God*, can make a long-term impact. Shorter cuttings are appropriate for younger grades.

How Should They Memorize

The sin nature rebels against being forced to do anything. Thus, if a young person feels they are under stress to commit something to memory, this will often lead to a "natural" attitude of rebellion. Teachers and parents have long been aware of the fact that young people enjoy things they do well. Because of this, baby steps that allow success are extremely important when memory work is required. If done incrementally, great things can be accomplished over time and the young person will feel a sense of accomplishment.

When it comes to factual knowledge, the single most important thing that the communicator can do is to make the fact come "alive." If we do not get excited about the learning of a fact or series of facts, it is highly doubtful that the learner will get excited about something that they have little or no interest in and which will involve work on their part. The listener must be able to see our passion about the subject matter. That is why one of the greatest enemies of learning is the communicator who acts each day as if he or she is giving out *S.O.S. – Same Old Stuff.* Often times that involves giving the background to something that we want listeners to understand. The Beatitudes were given during the midst of Roman rule over Israel, and yet Christ said, "Blessed are the peacemakers." The Gettysburg Address was delivered after people had heard a three-hour oration on the grounds of one of the great slaughters that occurred during all of American history. A brief sketch of the historical study that provides the skeleton for a Shakespeare play would certainly help the reader to better understand the content. Young people have a great desire to know why they must learn something, and often times, once we supply that necessary ingredient, the learning process is greatly aided.

A major way to accomplish success in memory work is through the use of the four *R*'s:

1. *Reinforcement* – Making sure that the students know the importance of what they are learning and why we want them to learn it.

2. *Recitation* – This may be verbally or on paper. Students quickly realize that they must work only to the level of that which we will inspect, and not for that which we just expect

3. *Reward* – The potential here is boundless. Verbal reward, notes to students, acknowledgment in front of family, class or youth group, ribbons, trophies, special meals, candy, or any one of a myriad number of things that students will work for. During the Second World War, one of the tortures that the Germans used against the Jews was to make them move a large pile of stones from one side of the road to the other. Upon completion, they were told to just move the stones back again. This literally broke both mind and spirit. Rewards offer perceived value, especially for younger students, whether it is a "star chart," a special sticker, or a jellybean. The communicator needs to have a "carrot" in front of the cart for the great majority of students.

4. *Review* – This is the step that is most often neglected. In youth groups, classes, and homes, continuity and review are often neglected. Repetition truly is a great tool. If we are striving for long-term results, we must strive for long-term memory. This is only accomplished through cumulative work where time is spent on review. Any parent whose children have been blessed by Ron Hamilton's "Patch the Pirate" tapes or CD's knows the effectiveness of Biblical lessons that are reviewed a multiplicity of times. That is why parents can complete the song "I will obey...the first time I'm told, I will obey right away," even though we never consciously sit down to listen to the tapes ourselves. Children learn these truths because they have reinforcement, recitation, and review as part of the process.

Facts are undoubtedly a major part of the learning process. If we can put feeling into them, it will help us as we try to shape future generations for the cause of Jesus Christ.

CHAPTER ELEVEN

Wisdom Through Wit

"A merry heart maketh a cheerful countenance: but by sorrow of the heart the spirit is broken." Proverbs 15:13

God's Word states that "a merry heart doeth good like a medicine." (Proverbs 15:22) Years ago, the earliest home health care providers (mothers) learned that the medicine would go down much easier with a "little bit of honey." Decades ago, Norman Cousins wrote the book *Anatomy of an Illness* in which he showed irrevocably that laughter not only caused pain to lessen but also helped in the healing process. Virtually everyone would agree that we enjoy a good "belly-laugh," and that good humor just makes us relax and feel better. The human race enjoys, as a rule, people who can make them smile and forget their troubles. This could be proved by the steady employment of folks ranging from the court jester of yesteryear to the comedians of today.

Since people enjoy smiling and laughing, and since many say it will lessen pain and cause increased receptivity to new concepts, why shouldn't Christian communicators be willing to use humor as a tool?

The theme of the book of Philippians is the "Joy in the Christian Life." Communicators of all generations have found that when people are happy it make for a more relaxed, less tense, and more receptive learning environment. The Philippian church was commanded to "rejoice...and again I say rejoice." (Philippians 4:4) This is also great advice for us today.

Learning is undoubtedly work, but to the chagrin of the "morbidly introspective ivory towerite," it can also be fun. After all, does not Galatians teach us that one of the fruits of the Spirit is joy? The effective Christian communicator should exhibit the joy of the Lord both in his person and in his teaching.

When using wit or humor, there are rules that must be remembered. First, if it is questionable – DON'T! It is imperative to always take the high road. Jokes about ethnic groups, bodily functions, and segments of society that live in opposition to the Word of God should be eliminated. God's Word states that it is not good to speak of those things which are "done in secret." (Ephesians 5:12) Secondly, it is best not to use humor that is biting or cutting about an individual person. Comments that the whole class or youth group might find hilarious can often wound a person for a lifetime.

Early in my teaching career, I was explaining an outside reading report project to a large class of about four hundred students. The project was simple and involved reading five hundred pages, typing a five-page report with a title page, punching the pages, placing it in a theme folder (choice of color left entirely up to the student), and turning it in by a certain date. After explaining this with incredible wit and clarity for about twenty minutes, I began to take questions from the class. Some of these questions were truly special (as in special ed!), and I did my very best to use my rapier-like wit to keep the class laughing as one question after another was dispatched with witticisms such as, "Don't laugh, you may have a child like that someday!" or "Once again we see the horrible results of rolling off a table onto concrete while an infant." I truly enjoyed myself.

Unfortunately, I totally failed to think about the fact that it was a college freshman class, the students didn't know me, and many were scared to death, more in need of an encouraging word than a biting comment. The lesson became real to me several years later during a special chapel service. A preacher asked for anyone who had a feeling of bitterness or resentment toward another person in the auditorium to go to that person and make it right. It was at that time that a student, one I did not know, came and apologized for the bitterness he had felt toward me for a number of years. He started by saying that when he was a freshman, I had offended him and made him feel stupid in front of his peers. Obviously, I immediately apologized for some statements that might be acceptable with a long-standing friendship or mentoring situation, but that could cause long-term hurt or even harm in the wrong situation.

Beyond these two areas lies a world of potential tools to add a touch of levity, joy, and happiness to a mentoring and modeling situation. Funny stories that happen to your family and yourself are always of interest. It doesn't matter if folks at times are laughing at us and not with us. The one area to guard against in this genre is the too-often repeated illustration that happened in one's youth. These will often be greeted with yawns on the second and third telling and will usually elicit comments about the Jurassic era, etc. As our children get older, we must also be careful to avoid causing undo embarrassment. God's Word enjoins us to "provoke not... to wrath." (Ephesians 6:4) And so, material that would be humorous to adults but humiliating to a teenager must be buried with immediacy.

The speaker with experience realizes that people often learn more easily when laughing. There is a comfort zone that makes one more amiable and receptive to outside impulses. There are many advantages from which the speaker will benefit if humor is used:

1) People will be participating with you.
2) People will be more relaxed.
3) People will listen to you and direct their thinking toward what you are saying.
4) People will give a greater level of concentration.
5) People will enjoy your time together (We do best in classes we enjoy).
6) People will better remember your words (both before and after the humor).
7) People will feel refreshed by a time of laughter and enjoyment.

Since most would readily agree that these principles have validity, the question is posed: "What type of humor should I use?" Jokes, personal illustrations, sarcasm, puns, and spontaneous humor all have their place in the speaker's pantheon of tests. As is true with so many areas of molding and mentoring, we should constantly be looking for things that would help us to be more effective in our appointed task. We all realize that what is funny to one is not funny to another, so we must always be careful and kind. (Ephesians 4:32)

Sources of Humor

One of the best sources of humorous stories is to be alert to the things that are happening around us in our daily lives. As a teacher, I immediately think of hilarious stories dealing with every aspect of Christian education. Where should you start - in the lunchroom, or perhaps with an ill-conceived birthday party? or how about the first time you ever took a group of kids on a field trip? I'll never forget reading the book *Proud to be a Teacher* by Bill Halloron. He talked about how his co-teacher had a bird in her room that got loose, flew into his room, and left a deposit on his head. The teacher, whose name was Stella, walked in, rubbed the bird droppings into his hair, and said, "The droppings are white, your hair is white. If I just rub it in, no one will know the difference. Now, just quiet down and teach your lesson..." Stories like that can't be improved upon.

True stories from the lives of others often bring a smile to our faces. Undoubtedly, those of us who are in the trenches with others enjoy hearing of the ridiculous situations our co-horts find themselves in. While we enjoy hearing those stories, we need to remember that those with whom we are communicating enjoy hearing stories from our lives.

A new source of humor that has opened up vast panoramas of new material at the click of a finger is the Internet. Whether your taste runs from red-neck jokes (Jeff Foxworthy), blonde jokes, or if you have a touch of macabre (DarwinAwards.com – those who improve the human race by removing themselves from the gene pool), there are so many new and excellent sources that we have never had easy access to before.

Since I teach the auditorium Bible class here at Lancaster, I am always looking for new humorous material. All it took was a single announcement to my class, and I began to receive copies of material that they had been forwarded via the Internet. On an average week, I receive at least fifteen pages of potential stories and jokes. While it is obvious that I cannot begin to use even a portion of this material, it has allowed me to collect several notebooks on material ranging from blondes to marriage. It is an unusual person who will not smile when hearing about the blonde who noticed that her house was on fire. She immediately and correctly called 911. After explaining the immediate need for help, she was asked by the operator, "How do we get to your house?" The blonde immediately replied, "Well, duh, the big red truck!"

Of course, if there were a single area that is the most fertile ground for good humor, it would have to be familial relationships. To maintain family peace, once again mother-in-law jokes and others of their ilk are often best left unsaid, or apologies may soon follow.

Other sources of humor include the *Clean Joke Book* series by Bob Phillips. There is a wide plethora of books that offer quips or quotes that can be used at the appropriate time!

When to Use Humor

Virtually always! Children, whether at home, school, or church, need encouragement and joy. In a world that is truly waxing "worse and worse," the Christian family is truly one of the few that has a reason to smile. If there is ever a principle to remember, it is that laughter is highly contagious.

Humor can be used to warm or prepare a group for a more serious matter. Humor can be used to lighten loads. Humor can be used to drive a point home or to teach a principle. But the operative thought is *can be...* Since humor and comedic timing certainly do not come naturally to everyone, it is apparent that it is a skill that must be practiced and perfected. The pregnant pause, coupled with a well-timed "Really..." is often enough to eradicate any icy front that may exist. Because of this, it is wise to look for proper places to use humor. Parents are sometimes especially susceptible to being so serious-minded that their own children don't even enjoy being with them. While it is certainly true that we want to teach lessons, truths, and principles, we must remember that if the listener does not enjoy listening, he or she will simply stop doing so.

Like the teachable moment, we must be alert to watch for the humorous instance. This brief period of time should not evolve into a litany of one-liners, but rather should simply be a time of mental pause or refreshment. There must be a warning given to the communicator not to get involved in an overly lengthy explanation or story that might lose the students' train of thought and lead them on an extended mental rabbit trail. To quote one well-known college fund-raising group, "A mind is a terrible thing to waste."

It is a joy to the communicator to see encouragement brought to the listener. The founders of *Reader's Digest*, the Wallaces, understood decades ago that interspersing humor between serious articles made their magazine more readable and interesting to the average American. The success of their philosophy speaks for itself.

It would be a wonderful thing for teachers and parents alike to bring more joy, smiles, and yes, good humor into the lives of those around us.

CHAPTER TWELVE

Wonders with Words

"A word fitly spoken is like apples of gold in pictures of silver."
Proverbs 25:11

Importance of Good Vocabulary

What a hammer is to a carpenter, or a brush is to a painter equates what words are to those whose calling it is to communicate truth. The end result of poorly-chosen words may result in confusion, embarrassment, or even insult.

Recent advertisements for programs such as Verbal Advantage © continually talk about the importance of a good vocabulary. But this is more than just a sales ploy. Dr. Johnson O'Connor of The Human Engineering Laboratory of Boston gave a vocabulary test to 100 young men who were studying to be executives. The results showed that after eight years every single man who had tested in the top ten percent was an executive, while not a *single* man in the lower 25% had become an executive. Truly, as the advertisement says, your words do "say it for you." While it is not our goal to display intelligence or to achieve status in the world, it is extremely important to be able to communicate truth with both clarity and power.

Carefully chosen words, especially when used to capsulate truth as in an epigram, are remembered and often achieve results long after the speaker has gone to his demise. Whether it was a Latin phrase uttered almost two millenniums ago like "Et tu, Brute," "V for Victory" during World War II, or Dr. Lee Roberson's "Everything rises and falls on leadership," quotes like these will undoubtedly be repeated until the trumpet sounds.

The words we use help create people's opinions about us. Choosing the right words will help people to decide whether or not we can be of help to them. Often we hear students say, "I know what I think, I just don't know how to say it." Unfortunately, according to Adam Robinson of the Princeton Review, "If they don't know how to say it, they usually don't know what they mean. We use words not just to speak but also to think." As we improve our vocabulary, we are helping ourselves in an attempt to communicate truth to those with whom the Lord allows us to come into contact.

Where do we start? What should we strive for? Let us challenge you to strive to look for the four "C's" of vocabulary. While the diamond trade looks for cut, carat, clarity, and color, the realtor looks for location, location, and location; we too need to look for some specifics when it comes to choosing the right words. S.I. Hoyakowa, who edited *Reader's Digest*'s *Use the Right Word – A Modern Guide to Synonyms,* said that to choose words well gives both illumination and delight. A single warning should be stated: bigger is not always better. Just because a word is long or officious sounding does not mean it is the best tool for the job.

If we want our child to wash the windows, it would be appropriate to say that there are dactyl grams that need to be

126

removed, but it probably would be more effective to say, "Please wash the fingerprints off the glass." And it is still better to call someone a friend than a trusty henchperson. The communicator will find that the large and unknown will soon have the audience in a state of pondiculation – oops! I meant yawning.

Challenging Words

As we enter the 21ˢᵗ century, we must remind ourselves that maybe we ought to look back for guidance to the time of the *McGuffey Reader* and *Blue-Backed Speller* instead of succumbing to the dumbing down of our culture and vocabulary. In *McGuffey's Fifth Eclectic Reader*, in just two paragraphs on page 34, the following words were found: *criterion, ambition, idolatry, subsidiary, promulgate, parricidal, despotism, reigned, surmount, opposition,* and *ubiquity.* The following page finds the students reading "Hamlet on Seeing the Skull of Yarick" and the following page finds Thomas Campbell's classic poem "Lord Ullin's Daughter."

Compared to this, we find young people today using language that has progressed beyond the gross and crude to the vulgar and obscene. It cannot be stressed enough that the books we read and the videos and television programs we watch will ultimately fuel a creative bank of vocabulary that we draw from. Programs like Fox Television's *The Simpsons* are lowering our vocabulary standards and introducing the crude and carnal into our society. Combining this source of words with the incredible amount of hours the average American child vegetates mindlessly, mentally nursing himself into a semi-comatose state, we can see how good vocabulary has almost been eradicated in our society today.

It is largely up to parents and teachers to introduce challenging words to the young. Oft times this is not done because we don't take the time to define or explain the word that would be the best choice rather than the acceptable choice. An example would be between using, "a careful researcher," when possibly meticulous or conscientious would be more exact. While Strunk and White may encourage not using a big word when a small one will do (*Elements of Style* by Strunk and White), what one needs to look for are words that best describe.

Unfortunately, in beginning with baby-talk and ending with talking down to students by over-simplification, all we are accomplishing is a mediocrity that seems to be set at a lower level with each ensuing year. One must be cognizant of the fact that the speed of the leader is generally the speed of the group. More importantly, those with whom we communicate will often pause or stop at the level below where we are. That is why we must aim high. Educators are already saying that the Generation X and the following Y Generation will be the first generations in history not to have attained the educational levels of their parents and grandparents - an amazing thought when one considers the wealth of resources now available to us.

Colorful Words

A painter with a vast array of colors to choose from realizes he can turn an evening sky from blue to cranberry to plum and then to indigo. So the orator can take a man through the seasons of life and age him. But here the choice of words can portray wildly divergent mental images. Think of words like elderly, patriarchal, and venerable, and compare them to words like senile, antiquated, and doddering, to see what the emphasis on the negativity of aging can do to the mental picture art forms of the aged subject.

Effective speakers and writers alike have learned that colorful words can captivate an audience. When describing flowers, one could say that the flower bed was very pretty, or he could describe it by saying that Mrs. Smith had labored over her garden until it seemed to burst in an explosion of color that seemed to embrace their allotted space with an effusive ebullience that almost took one's breath away. Sin could be described as being bad or horrible, but the use of words like repugnant, revolting, disgusting, and loathsome certainly elevate feelings of disgust toward the offense.

Since so much of learning is visually accented, the molder and mentor must realize the importance of creating word pictures. Warren Wiersbe details the many times that the Scriptures use mental imagery in his book *Teaching and Preaching with Imagination*. The most obvious example of this is seen in the parables. We need to describe with clarity and color so that the listener will never be in confusion as to our meaning. The words are available if we will just take the time to search them out and place them in the proper place.

Clear Words

The wisest man who ever lived said, "A word fitly spoken is like apples of gold..." Clarity comes from choosing the right word for the right audience. Don't obfuscate or hide the truth. When sharing the story of Goliath with an elementary child, size could be described as huge, giant, immense, colossal, and even taken from classical literature, gargantuan. But for the elementary mind, it should be clear that these are synonyms and are being used merely to emphasize the size of David's foe.

One must judge carefully each teaching or preaching opportunity to be sure that all verbiage used is clearly understood by the listener. It must never be forgotten that, prior to retention, we always will find comprehension. Clarity is as necessary to the speaker as water is to a garden. Clear explanation and description will allow the thought process to grow and flower into concepts, principles, and truths.

A clear description will often result in the proverbial light going on and an appreciative "I understand now" being uttered. Clear descriptions, like clear directions, are a necessity if we are to get the listener to the destination that we have in mind.

Concise Words

The old adage says, "Say what you mean and mean what you say." Ephesians 5:16 says to "redeem the time." Undoubtedly, all of us can remember being in a classroom or office meeting where it seemed as if the one who held the floor was meandering around the stated subject almost as if he were afraid to approach it directly, lest he be rebuffed. The listeners, lulled by non-essential droning, soon lose both interest and patience and once again defeat has been snatched from the jaws of victory.

One of the quickest ways to bore a listener into mental oblivion is to leave him in a mental quandary by using words that do not clearly, exactly, and quickly show him your intent and direction. The vagaries of the English language beg for conciseness. To say that the man was very big does not imply the conciseness of his "towering frame" or even his "obvious obesity."

So when choosing a word, remember our four C's of *challenging, colorful, clear,* and *concise.*

Word Resources

Unfortunately, for the busy or those who would disdain extra effort, there is no such thing as a vocabulary pill. Furthermore, it has clearly been proven that osmosis is quite ineffective, no matter how many books we choose to sleep with or on. How then does the person who has decided to become better equipped verbally go about increasing his repertoire of "tools"?

It could be said that what we must do is stop, look, and listen. If we are aware of the fact that words are our tools and that we can freely and somewhat easily add them to our verbal "tool bag," we will soon add to our resources.

Reading is unquestionably the greatest avenue toward an expounded vocabulary. Listen to the descriptive powers of a few authors. Papani gives a unique and vivid picture of the manger scene in his book *Life of Christ*:

> The green grass, the long, slim blades were cut down by the scythe; and with the grass the beautiful flowers in full bloom- white, red, yellow, blue. They withered and dried and took on the one dull color of hay. Oxen dragged back to the barn the dead plunder of May and June. And now that grass has become dry hay and those flowers, still smelling sweet, are there in the Manger to feed the slaves of man...this is the real stable where Jesus was born. The filthiest place in the world was the first room of the only Pure Man ever born of woman. The Son of Man, who was to be devoured by wild beasts calling themselves men, had as His first cradle the manger where the animals chewed the cud of the miraculous flowers of Spring...

Now listen to Dana in the classic *Two Years Before the Mast* as he describes the captain. *"And he began laying the blows upon his back, swinging half round between each blow to give it full effect. As he went on, his passion increased and he danced about the deck."* Or O. Henry in "The Green Door" as he describes a girl awakening from a faint: *"The frank, gray eyes, the little nose, turning pertly outward; the chestnut hair, curling like the tendrils of a pea vine...but the face was woefully thin and pale."* The list could go on, ranging from the classics like Twain with his jumping frogs or Melville with his mighty whale. It is the authors and wordsmiths who will expand our consciousness of new words.

Beyond reading on a wide scale, there are books that can be of help. A synonym dictionary is a great place to start reading. It will give us comparisons, contrasts, and contexts in digestible style. Others, like Norman Lewis with *Word Power Made Easy,* Dr. Wilfred Funk, with his many books such as *Six Weeks to Words of Power* and *30 Days to a More Powerful Vocabulary*, act as teachers willing to take us up the gradient to a better vocabulary. *Reader's Digest* has "Word Power," modeled after its popular vocabulary page, "It Pays to Increase your Word Power." Other books include *1100 Words You Need to Know* by Bromberg and Gordon, and, of course, there are a wide variety of specialized and eclectic books such as *Where In the Word?* which tells unusual stories behind ordinary words (author David Muschell).

Of course, a dictionary and thesaurus are invaluable tools for the educated mind. My father once told me that if he were to surrender all but two books, he would keep first his Bible, and secondly, his Webster's 1828 dictionary. A dictionary should be an old friend and a valued tool. It will unfold meaning in words and allow them to express their complete essence and meaning if we will use this great tool.

While vocabulary cards and lists are in all probability a necessary evil that do contain benefits on the elementary level, for the adult professional, one will probably find the study of roots, prefixes, and suffixes to be of a far greater value. These can also be extremely advantageous to the middle school and high school student. In many ways, a minimal study of Latin and Greek stems and prefixes will equip the reader with word "keys" that will unlock a multiplicity of meanings in both years and words to come.

Above all, we must be willing to exert the effort to describe truths and principles in a way that can be easily visualized and remembered. Years after his death, people still quote the chapel sayings of Dr. Bob Jones, Sr. "The door to success swings on the hinges of opposition" and "Don't be a rabbit chaser" are both picturesque and powerful. More importantly, they are remembered, quoted, and are still helping to teach truths to a new generation.

We need to challenge ourselves to be sure that we clothe truth in verbal garments that are fitting, appropriate, and yes, even sometimes beautiful.

Techniques for Teaching and Increasing Word Power

It could be said that we need to find a system that we like and then work it. Like exercise, dieting, and memorization, there are many ways to accomplish a single stated purpose or goal. The key is not to find 20-30 ways or even 20-30 books and then advise or look at them; rather, the key is to find a tool and use it.

The excellent interactive books that are inexpensive and readily available are certainly a good place to start. It will suffice to say that the key is to do more than start the book.

Others have chosen to learn a word a day. If this is a goal, using this new word in a sentence daily for a week will certainly help to place it more firmly in the bank of memory.

Games where synonyms or antonyms must be named are helpful. For either parents or teachers, a new "word of the day" is an excellent tool for teaching something new. Schoolteachers should seek to teach English words, and Sunday school teachers should teach Bible words. Truly words are wonderful assets that we cannot afford *not* to learn, deploy, and teach.

To emphasize the importance of clear communication, here are thoughts on the importance of words from giants of the past:

Thought is impossible without words. – John Dewey

With words we govern men. – Disraeli

Each word was at first a stroke of genius. – Emerson

Syllables govern the world. – Selden

Language! The blood of the soul! – Oliver Wendoll Holmes

Words are the instruments that make thought possible. – Judd

Most men paint, fish or collect stamps. My hobby is the dictionary.
        – Ashurst

Words are the soul's ambassadors. – Howell

Words are the voice of the heart. – Confucius

The unaccountable spell that lurks in a syllable. – Hawthorne

Words are the dress of thoughts. – Chesterfield

Words are the most powerful drug used by mankind. – Kipling

The use of the right word is more important than the right argument.
        – Joseph Conrad

Our words have wings. – Eliot

Every word was once a poem. – Emerson

What a man cannot clearly state he does not know. – British

So long as the language lives the nation lives too. – Czech proverb

Language is the armory of the human mind. – Coleridge

Words are the body of thought. – Carlyle

Whose words all ears took captive. – Shakespeare

Words are the pegs to hang ideas on . – Beecher

How strong an influence in well-placed words! – Chapman

Words are the signs of ideas. – Samuel Johnson

We rule men with words. – Napoleon

Language is the immediate gift of God. – Noah Webster

Good words are worth much and cost little. – Herbert

Words are the only things that last forever. – Hazlitt

Words are the very stuff and process of thought. – British

Thoughts that breathe and words that burn. – Gray

Words...may become alive and walk up and down in the hearts of men.
    – British

Clearness is the most important matter in the use of words.
    – Quintillian

Choice word and measure phrase above the reach of ordinary men.
    – Wordsworth

The only thing I would whip schoolboys for is not knowing English.
    – Churchill

Language is the dress of thought. – Samuel Johnson

Words are wise men counters. – Hobbes

A word travels farther than a man. – German

Language is the archives of history. – Emerson

Words are the dress of our thoughts which should no more be presented in rags, tatters, and dirt than your person should. – Chesterfield

CHAPTER THIRTEEN
Questions with Quality

"Hast thou entered into the springs of the sea? or hast thou walked in the search of the depth?" Job 38:16

Teaching and communication are far more than just the dispersing of knowledge. One who mentors and molds realizes that the student or hearer must be mentally stimulated in order to help the hearer desire to gain understanding. Furthermore, one can use questions to cause thought processes to occur which will lead to the hearer's desire to discover more about a given subject or to gain an enlarged understanding of a subject. This is best illustrated by thinking back to the person or event that first piqued our interest in a certain subject. Maybe it was a question about World War II that led my dad to check out Cornelius Ryan's classic *The Longest Day* and give it to me as a sixth grader. That book led to a lifelong love of history. In recent days, the reading of the classic adventure book *Into Thin Air* by Krakaeur led me to read at least two other books about the 1996 Everest disasters, as well as the autobiography of the greatest mountaineer of all time, Reinhold Messner.

It was Socrates who said over two millennia ago that the teacher should not talk. He said, "The teacher asks questions and the student talks." Socrates felt that proper questioning will make the listener conscious of his ignorance or lack of knowledge in a given area and will guide him to seek out truth. Obviously, there must be a commonality or basis of discussion prior to questioning. If you will, we must first get on the same page. The responsibility for this lies entirely in the communicator's court. Young people often don't know what they don't know! We must remember that an excellent definition of teaching is "to cause to learn."

The Importance of Asking Good Questions

In a day where society seems to produce the human equivalent of lemmings, leaders need to realize that they must provoke students to both thought and to good, autonomous thinking. If a student does not think, he does not learn. Questions are directed at getting the student's mind involved in the area pre-chosen by the communicator. A parent might ask, "How could instant obedience save your life in the future?" A teacher might ask, "Why is it important to have listening skills?" A Sunday School teacher could ask, "How does your behavior now affect your future?"

It is extremely important to show the students that they can and must think on their own. Literally, we must at times force others to think. When deciphering the best way to do this, we must make students learn on their own. This is difficult because it is almost always easier just to tell the students ourselves instead of allowing them to discover on their own. Obviously, when it comes to moral bylaws such as the Ten Commandments, we have a responsibility to teach. Rather, we are suggesting the giving of guidance leading to self-discovery. It is also extremely important to point out that we are "molders of dreams" and "casters of vision." All too often, we confuse the students saying *I can't* with what in reality is *I won't*. While it is true that we "can't fly," it usually is not true that we can't "get it." With desire, help, and motivation, they usually can.

Application of Truths

"Why do I need to learn this?" is a refrain that is often stated and almost always thought. The true molder or mentor will always be looking for practical applications that can be understood and seen as relevant by the hearer. There should be a time in the lesson where the hearer understands how a specific item applies to his life. This is the crucial moment when the proverbial light bulb turns on. When the lesson becomes connected to the machinery of living, change is then brought about. Once this connection is established, it becomes far easier to maintain the student's interest, attention, and focus on the truth at hand. This is why testing and questioning over previously shared material is so very important. The listener must understand that there is an accountability involved. "I did not hear you" or "I did not understand" lack in both originality and validity as far as answers are concerned.

When to Ask Questions

A credo that has been oft quoted is, "The active mind is a questioning mind." This infers that when the mind is actively involved, questions will be both asked and answered. Teachers have long been alert to the students who never ask questions in class. Those students who hide tortoise-like behind blank stares are usually headed for academic difficulties.

The Sunday School or day school teacher needs to ask questions at the opening of the class period. It is imperative to get the mental wheel turning, and even turning in the proper direction.

These questions will sharpen understanding of a predisposed direction as well as cast light on implications or problems that might arise during a certain path of inquiry.

Once the class is underway, it is crucial that questions continue to be asked to see if the proper level of understanding is being reached. These questions will also serve to accomplish a myriad of other tasks for the teacher. Questions can reinforce a truth, summarize a body of work, encourage the class that they are learning the material, and enhance explanation. While it is important to ask students to define a fact or truth, it is of tantamount importance that the communicator checks to see if the student's attitude, paradigm, and world view are being affected in a Christo-centric way.

Obviously, when a difficult concept is being explained, it would be appropriate to ask a question verbally and have the entire class write down their understanding of the proper answer. A quick perusal of these answers will allow the teacher to immediately know exactly where the listener stands in relation to the truth. A parent or youth director could pose ethical questions as to what should be done under $a+b+c$ circumstances. It is also very enlightening to ask students why they have given a certain response. If the logistics are convoluted or have strayed from a Biblical basis, this affords an excellent teaching opportunity as well as a chance to get our "charges" back on the correct track. At times like this, young people are often given to sharing opinions, and this represents an excellent opportunity to see how they think.

At the close of a class or lesson, it is also wise to use questions in two different venues: first, to provoke and challenge as they leave. This obviously takes more forethought than the ever popular "Class is dismissed." It is also appropriate to finish a segment of material with review questions. To retrace a mental

140

journey will allow the communicator to re-emphasize key truths. This gives us yet another chance to let the students know what we think is most important. Realizing that students will never "learn it all," we need to predicate where the heaviest volume of work and study will be placed. If this is not done, the student who has been passively absorbing at a constant rate will ultimately be bewildered as he attempts to classify truth or facts on some type of hierarchical system.

A class corporately or a mind singly is a living organism. It is either progressing or regressing. The only way to verify the direction is by asking questions. Every parent who has taught a child a specific set of facts, whether it was a times table or some of America's early colonial history, has found the necessity of review questions. It is only by a continual asking of the same question that the repeated focus is brought to bear. Then the truths slide, albeit sometimes slowly, from the short-term memory bank to the area that we euphemistically call long-term memory.

Asking Effective Questions

As creative communicators, we realize that it is our job to stimulate the student to discover meaning and truth. If we are going to inspire and motivate the listener, we quickly realize that our focus must be on the listener and not on ourselves. One of the most important books ever written on communication is *How to Win Friends and Influence People* by Dale Carnegie. This book, while over half a century old, is just as applicable today as when it was written because it is still true today that we need to learn to ask questions, and then we must be good listeners. Proper questions will create discovery on the end of both asker and receiver. The leader will focus on the truth being taught and will work with the listener to help him as he searches for meaning in this discovery process. It is of utmost importance to realize that the teacher-student relationship is in no way, shape, or form an adversarial relationship. Rather, it is a situation where one takes a novice on a journey that he has already taken. This path is one that we, but not they, are familiar with; thus, we must constantly be checking to see if they are still with us as we move forward.

In asking the right type of questions, we need to realize that it is almost always best to require more than a "yes" or "no" answer. This will entail using questions that involve words like *how* or *why*. When we realize that questioning is part of the warp and woof of teaching and not merely a device of teaching, we will realize the need to keep questions coming.

Effective questions must be easily understood rather than wordy. Questions should also be inquisitive rather than accusative. "When do you think the next plane will leave?" is acceptable, whereas "Do any of your planes ever leave on time?" is accusative and immediately puts someone on the defensive. When the communicator feels tired, harassed, peeved, or even unappreciated, he sometimes responds in a way that engenders hostility. Proverbs 16:21b makes it clear that the "sweetness of a man's lips" increases learning.

Effective questions will create new paradigms and be definitive in purpose. Therefore, it is wise to prepare questions in advance to arriving at certain crucial points in a lesson. The listener then will often arrive at an answer prior to its having been given by the communicator. Socrates felt that truth was in the pupil's power to find. He felt that his questions would steer the pupil slowly and maybe even imperceptibly toward a preordained region of truth or thought. Although this may sound laborious at first, this thorough approach will create a needed solution that people will want and need to seek out, and most importantly, will create in the listener the desire to find exactly that which you want them to find.

Getting the Listener Involved

As questions are being asked, it is important for the listener to realize that you have a genuine interest and excitement regarding the topic at hand. Some fear that a deeper treatment of a subject necessitates the induction of boredom. While it is true that real intellectual effort can be exhausting (remember standardized tests), proper preparation from the teacher can negate many feared consequences (i.e. semi-comatose states, etc.).

To get a listener involved, it is mandatory to always begin with the known. To go from the known toward the unknown is far less daunting than attempting to get one to take a leap into what has been a mental void or black hole. This is why people so often get lost or just "don't get it." Often while taking that first step from the familiar to the new, it is good to give the listener time to think. This acts as an acclimatization time with the new stimuli that are now present. After connections have been made, it is extremely effective to ask a question and then to completely stop talking. This often drives a person toward a pre-ordained conclusion. This tactic has been used for years in the sales realm, where it is effective in getting a buyer to come to the seller's point of view. It is the communicator's job to apply the stimuli whereby thinking must take place.

When answers are forthcoming, it is crucial to remember that we praise right answers and help those with wrong answers to find the truth. Do not become overt in the criticism of a wrong conclusion, lest you drive the student into a reticent clam-like attitude in the future. There is almost always something positive that can be praised about an answer. At times, questions will need to be restated or even made easier. It is important to note that we enjoy things we do well and that a steady diet of failure will lead to a "bunker" mentality and ultimately to surrender in that particular venue.

Another crucial way to use questions is to be sure to allow the hearers time to ask questions. These questions can be academic or non-academic. Since we are all teachers and those around us need to continually learn just as we do, we need to create an environment that is question-friendly. When the young child asks, "Why do we have to use soap in the bath?" a wonderful opportunity has been created to talk about the human body, cleanliness, germs, disease, etc. It must be noted that a three-year-old certainly would not need a thirty-minute treatise on any or all of the above. Hopefully short, trenchant answers for the young will be forthcoming, although this is always more difficult with questions such as, "Mom, where is God?"

If a question does arrive at the wrong time, such as in the middle of devotions or at a church service, give a definitive time when the question could be properly asked. It is also wise to jot down the question yourself and bring it up at a later time to foster a questioning spirit. Teachers in both church and school must understand the necessity of finding answers to questions posed in class. Few things will garner more respect than to have a teacher come back the following class time, re-address the question, and give an answer. Respect is often squandered when the communicator says he will find the answer and then fails to do so. The listeners will ask questions with much greater frequency if they truly believe that if questions are asked at the proper time, they will be answered.

Examples of Thought-Provoking Questions

It is probably not necessary to state, but in the educational testing area, it is wise to use a variety of question types. Fill in the blank, true or false, matching, multiple-choice, and essay all result in different thought processes to derive a solution. Just as it is true in exercising to make muscles work in different ways, so it is true with the mind.

When a communicator is trying to ask questions that will lead to a knowledge or understanding of truth, there are two distinct avenues that can be taken in the questioning process. First, one can put the listener into a situation where he needs to make a response. An example would be to ask a youngster, "If someone says to you, 'You need to try this cigarette so you can decide for yourself whether you like it,' what will your answer be?" This tool is extremely important for the leader who knows the perils that populate the road of life. It is extremely wise to help young people or young Christians to think through the correct answer prior to being forced in the wrong direction by peer pressure or by a decision based on impulse. This can help young people to realize that "The heart is deceitful about all things and desperately wicked..." Thus we need to ask ourselves what would God have us to do in a certain situation.

A second approach would be to offer a dilemma or problem and ask how they would solve it. It is sometimes easier to come to a proper conclusion when we are outside the equation ourselves. This allows us to dissipate the problems of ego and pride that often lead us in the wrong direction. Upon the listener's reaching the proper conclusion, it is appropriate to immediately press for personal application.

Questions are valuable tools that must be included in the arsenal of those who hope to develop "polished shafts" in their ministry.

CHAPTER FOURTEEN

Power Through Principles

"Hear, ye children, the instruction of a father, and attend to know understanding. For I give you good doctrine, forsake ye not my law." Proverbs 4:1-2

Today there are many who shirk the teaching of home, church, and school because of its so-called irrelevance. Unfortunately, this is partially due to those in charge of communicating truth. While all parents understand the necessity of children obeying because we ask them to, it is extremely advantageous for them to understand the principles behind the command. It is true that we need to mentor our charges and prepare them for the real world. Undoubtedly, this is best done when decisions are principle-based. The only principles that are perfectly pure and sure (Psalm 12:6,7) are found in the pages of the Word of God. It will stand us in good stead if we adhere to principles that are *"sound words."* These words, the Bible says, are "quick and powerful, sharper than any two-edged sword, piercing even to the dividing asunder of soul and spirit, and of the joints and marrow, and is a discerner of the thoughts and intents of the heart." (Hebrews 4:12) Because of this fact, the principles taught in the church, the Christian school, or the godly home truly do equip the hearer for the real world.

Unfortunately, due to the multitudinous demands on our time, these life-changing principles are often neglected. In many ways, these principles were a priority issue in early Americana. A brief perusal of the *McGuffey Readers* or even the original Webster's dictionary shows the importance of God-honoring principles. Since that time, enemies ranging from divorce to materialism to humanism and even hedonism have progressively widened the gap between what God wants and what we are. But Matthew 6:33 is still inspired, and we need to teach principles that will help the listener to "*seek first*" the things of God.

Principles to Apply

It is the living of and by principles that makes one a disciplined person in life. Although books like *The Disciplined Life* by Taylor are extremely helpful, the single most important lesson is to get those we have influence over to realize that they must choose to please God and to live by the precepts of His Word. It has been said that there are but two choices on the shelf, pleasing God and pleasing self. So while the ultimate goal of discipline is self-discipline, it must be understood that we are going to be choosing either King Jesus or King Self. Little things certainly do count, for each and every choice in life will ultimately show subservience to one of these two monarchs.

It is of extreme importance for the younger generation to realize that little things do count. God's Word says that the little foxes spoil the vine, and never has this been truer than the generation in which we now live. The discipline involved in the family and school alike, as wide-ranging as hairstyles and language to make-up and dating, are helping to shape the character of the

148

next generation. Those who think that their "rights" are being taken away need to genuflect on what it was like to learn in the one room schoolhouse where rod and ferrule were used with impunity. The inability and distaste for submission to authority is a result of sin nature, pride, and the battle against the principle of submission. Thus, it is extremely important for those that God has placed in charge to hold the standards high and to continually reinforce Biblical principles that ultimately will make a major difference both now and down the road in the practitioner's life. These principles are even being touted in the mainstream press today under the title of values. Hence we hear about value-centered education, and authors like William Bennett are suddenly in high demand. This is solely due to the fact that the pendulum has swung so far from our Biblical moorings that even the liberals realize that conservative judge Robert Bork might be correct in that we are "slouching toward Gomorrah."

It is important for the communicator to teach that mistakes, sins, and incorrect action all have self-contained consequences. God's Word states it succinctly when it says, "For they have sown the wind, and they shall reap the whirlwind:" (Hosea 8:7) We can certainly see this played out on the following chart:

Smoking smokeless tobacco	*lung, mouth cancer*
Drug abuse	*drug addiction, hepatitis*
Fornication, hedonism, homosexuality	*AIDS and many other sexually transmitted diseases*
Beer, wine, hard liquor	*hangovers, drunkenness, drunk driving, alcoholism, cirrhosis of the liver, DTD's*

However, we could also add:

Slothfulness   *ruin of reputation, possibly a life*
                                    on the dole

Dishonesty   *loss of trust, a character opposite*
                                    of the one called truth

The list could go on for pages. Therefore, when an attribute that goes in opposition to Biblical principles is seen, it must be dealt with. People can learn from their mistakes. But the most difficult mistakes to deal with are those that have become entrenched in character and have become, by force of habit, habitual actions. We have a tremendous responsibility to *"train up a child,"* for as the twig is bent, so grows the tree. While no problem is too big for God, one does not need to study the federal prison system long to see the enormous problem recidivism causes.

Powerful Practical Principles

After reading this next section on powerful principles, we have no doubt that the average response will be, "Of course!" or, "Obviously." Even the University of Michigan has an institute called Values in Action with an attendant website and questionnaire at the following address: www.positivepsychology.org/strengths (per. *USA Today* 1/9/02). The Institute mentions character strengths like love, gratitude, hope, and kindness - certainly all subjects that God's Word has much to say about. God's Word is the final authority in all matters of both faith and practice. Practice deals with the way that we are to live our lives. Of course, the new nature gives us the desire to do the right thing, as is clearly taught in Philippians 2:13, which says, "For it is God which worketh in you both to will and to do of his good pleasure." So what principles are God's good pleasure for us? The Bible principles like honesty (Romans 12:17), purity (I John 3:3), servanthood (Matthew 25:21), and doing our best (I Corinthians 10:31), are among the principles that should be shaping and making the lives of those in our charge. It cannot be underestimated how many of these Bible truths are better caught than taught. Those in our care need to see us always telling the truth, living a life of purity, being willing to be a servant, and truly giving our all to the Master. While it is by the "foolishness of preaching" that men are saved, we must remember that it is also effective to see a sermon preached as well. As a young man growing up, my mother taught me these verses: "Thou shalt not bear false witness..." and "...all liars shall have their part in the lake which burneth with fire and brimstone, which is the second death." But I also learned a great deal from watching my mother, as she was a personal sterling example of always doing exactly what she said and never allowing there to be any question about the veracity of her words. God's Word says to let your *yea* be *yea* and your *nay* be *nay*. Those around us surely need to see this exemplified in our lives as well.

While Biblical principles need to start in one's life and heart, there are other principles that are group-oriented. The principle of submission to authority and its attendant issue of accountability can certainly be based on the verse: "Obey them that have the rule over you, and submit yourselves: for they watch for your souls, as they that must give account..." (Hebrews 13:17) This, of course, is fought by the old nature that pushes us continually in the areas of pride, disobedience, and self will. Other principles that certainly should be broached would include doing one's share of the work, teamwork, tolerance and understanding of others, and even a willingness to listen to the ideas of others. As Christian leaders, we do need to explain the differentiation between loving

151

the sinner and hating the sin. The religion of humanism expects us to accept every factor in the rapid declension of morals as yet another step of the "progression" of mankind. The listener must comprehend that, like Christ, we must separate the person and the actions; for while God loves the world, it is still sin that separates us from Him. While we are ambassadors for Christ (II Corinthians 5:20), we are still in an alien land and, like an ambassador, must go through training to receive proper protocol. So we also have to train those that God has placed in our care so that they do not disappoint the King they are serving. One cannot underestimate the power of saying that the reason something ought to be done is because it is a Biblically based principle. This gives power and credibility to a command that is unequalled by any other source.

Principle-based living can also be taught through any and all curriculum. Since it is by Him that all things consist, we need to clearly delineate God's place in whatever we are teaching. If teaching one how to mow a lawn, God's way is to do things decently and in order. This same principle would obviously apply to cleaning the garage, weeding the flowers, or straightening one's bedroom. This is certainly a principle I have stressed prior to white-glove inspection of college dorms for over twenty years. It is interesting to note that some pastors have made it a point not to hire a staff member unless he can first go down and inspect the cleanliness of the prospect's car. While some may think this to be overly invasive, it is quite possible that this may be a reflection of the work space, classroom, or desk in future days.

God is a God of order. In the field of academics, we can see this demonstrated through a variety of principles. In math-related courses, we need to teach that the end does *not* justify the means. Therefore, young people are taught to show their work. It could rightly be said that in many ways the process is as important as the ultimate outcome. Were this not to be the case, we would certainly be much fonder of a degree mill than the 128 class credits being earned on site at an institution of higher learning. Mathematics can also teach us principles in the areas of diligence and consistency. Finally, math will clearly validate the Bible principle of "line upon line, precept upon precept."

In the field of science, the Bible principle of persistence is seen time and time again. The passages referring to a hand cleaving to the sword (II Samuel 23:10) and taking the plough and not looking back (Luke 9:62) certainly were exhibited by inventors like Edison, who never failed in his work on the light bulb, but rather found multiplied hundreds of ways that a light bulb would stay lit. We can also see God's power and might exhibited through Creation and even the briefest study of the awesome size of the universe. We see attention to detail in the molecular structure, the ribbons of DNA, and the individuality of each person- yes, even each fingerprint. Hopefully, we can also teach courage and a willingness to try new things as we look at those who stepped where others had not been. This could range from the first inoculations by Jenner, explorations in the field of radium by Madame Curie, or even Glenn Shepherd and Neil Armstrong, who truly traveled where none had ever traveled before. The analogies to the Christian life are both numerous and obvious.

In the field of English, we should start with the importance of being able to communicate God's Word. One can't help but wonder how many times the beautiful clarity of the Gospel has been befuddled by a simple lack of orderliness or organization. Words are the tools that God has given us to express the truth of salvation. As a carpenter needs to be adept with hammer, saw, and drill, so we too need to teach others how to communicate God's truth. My college president stated that the most important class one could take was English. It is certainly true that our daily walk and conversation will not reflect much on our background of physics, algebra, biology, or calculus. But even a short conversation will readily reveal our mastery of our mother tongue. We can certainly use the Master Communicator of all time as our example in this arena. Just direct your attention to Matthew 5-7 for an illustration of principle-based communication bathed in love and presented in clarity. Truly, He is the Master Teacher.

History, of course, should be presented as *HIS story*. The applications in history are extremely easy to make, for God's laws are illustrated and reiterated on the canvas of humanity. Those we are privileged to teach must be made aware of the fact that while experience is an effective teacher, it is not always the best teacher. We need to experience riding a bike, but we can learn from the travails of those who have experienced drug addiction or the horrible ramifications of unfaithfulness. History is redolent with those who have obeyed God and those who have not. The theme of the book of Deuteronomy is " A Blessing for Obedience and a Curse for Disobedience." God has not rescinded this because of the onset of a new millennium. Other principal truths that can be drawn from the pages of history and biography include the importance of choosing whom to sit under (Psalm 1) and whom to walk with (Proverbs 13:20).

Another obvious area of emphasis would be the Biblical principle of sowing and reaping. While the world exploits a reckless abandon in pursuit of pleasure and the "feel good" mentality, it cannot be overly emphasized that there are so many livable lessons to be gleaned from the lives of legends. Because of this, biographical material is always a verdant source for teaching principles.

Of course, the subject that has long been hailed as the queen of academia is the study of the Word of God. Sir Walter Scott, while lying on his deathbed, said, "Bring me the Book." His aid said, "Sir, you have thousands of books." Scott answered and made it clear that for such a time, there was only one Book - the Word of God. Truly a man could be well educated and never traverse beyond the pages of God's Word. Its principles are the secret to a productive and happy life. Continual mining will consistently turn up new gems, almost as if with each new search, the Holy Spirit, Who was given to guide us into all truth, allows a new vein of truth to be revealed.

Application of Principles

The communicator is constantly on the watch for what could be called "the teachable moment." This is the time when the application is made and the pertinence is realized. If the student can see and learn the lesson himself from the collected facts and principles, it is even more effective in the long run. One must be careful not to use peers as negative examples, such as, "See what happened to Danny when he didn't obey?" A few times when teachable moments seem to continually pop up would include times of games or competition. Everything from following the rules to treating others with kindness beg to be taught in this environment. During school, recess gives an excellent opportunity to teach concerning leisure time. Field trips certainly bring to mind deportment and the image that we portray to the world around us.

Other learning times arrive when we see courage profiles in any genre. Early Americans, from Daniel Boone to Lewis and Clarke, were the embodiment of courage, bravery, and fortitude. Our pampered society, which would equate a difficult night away from home as one spent at Motel 6 rather than at the Hilton, has much to learn from our predecessors. There were those who stood for truth even when it went diametrically against the tide of public opinion. Early proponents of the heliocentric theory (Copernicus, Galileo, etc.) braved being called heretics because of their view of the solar system. What a tremendous lesson for those who realize that they will be rebuked and ridiculed because of their testimony for Christ. How much more important is it that we be willing to stand for eternal principles! Paul, Stephen, John, and, of course, the Lord Jesus stood firm in the minority opinion and refuted the great tide of public opinion. Having done all, they stood, even though ultimately it cost them their lives. The pantheons of martyrs called from numerous sources are valid heroes that should draw our attention. Unfortunately, the youth of today are far more familiar with Michael Jordan and Kobe Bryant than with William Carey and Hudson Taylor.

Questions are also critical in seeing truth applied and principles made practical. Questions such as, "How should this have been done differently?" "What would be the Bible way to approach this?" and, "How could Christ have received honor through this situation?" all serve as powerful teaching tools. Sole memorization and recitation of facts will fail us in our goal to develop the mind of Christ. C.S. Lewis stated rather succinctly that "education without [Christian] values, as useful as it is, seems rather to make a more clever devil." We must remember the clarity of the statement found in God's Word which states, "for of him, and through him, and to him, are all things!" (Romans 11:36)

Above all else, it must be a continual thrust in our mentoring process to plow deeply the principles that are found in the Word of God. Someone must take seriously the command to "train up a child in the way he should go." Unfortunately, sometimes there is more effort placed on the training of the family canine than there is on the children that God has blessed us with to nurture and train. Bob Jones Sr. said, "You will be someday what you are now becoming." We ought to ask ourselves, *What are we helping those children to become whom God has placed under our watch care?* The wisest man who ever lived said that "iron sharpeneth iron, so a man sharpeneth the countenance of his friend." (Proverbs 27:17) As we reflect what Dr. Luke said under the inspiration of the Holy Spirit in chapter 2 verse 52, we ought to be challenged to use principles to challenge our charges to grow in a balanced way as the supreme Example did almost 2,000 years ago.

CHAPTER FIFTEEN
Revival of Responsibility

"Let no man despise thy youth; but be thou an example of the believers, in word, in conversation, in charity, in spirit, in faith, in purity." I Timothy 4:12

When was the last time you heard about a young person that is a "responsible young man"? Has it been a long while? Maybe that is because leaders no longer expect or emphasize this issue of responsibility. Our society today bemoans the fact that absenteeism is up, days for sickness seem especially prevalent on Mondays and Fridays (thus creating three day weekends), and the average worker has no more intention of working a solid eight hours than he has intention of going to space on the next shuttle mission. Why is this? Perceptions certainly affect performance, and we must let those in our care realize that we expect a high level of performance. There is no doubt among sociologists that many graphs charting the progress of America's youth resemble nothing so much as a giant slide. Unfortunately, as those in authority expect and require less, the results are exactly as expected. While we must guard against humanistic theories that essentially proclaim "whatever the mind of man can conceive that man can achieve," we need to seek to instill the indomitable "can do," "won't quit" spirit that was so essential in the birthing and developing of the United States of America. Our forefathers instilled in their progeny the attitude that "*I can* makes a great man." One historian said that it was not unusual for the early pioneers to attempt the impossible and expect to get it done before lunch. What a far cry from the sniveling irresponsibility often seen in today's youth. Recognizing that we ought to have a goal to be training responsible, hardworking young people who are goal-driven and strive for excellence, the question must be posed, *How do we develop this?*

God's Word says in Psalm 16:3 "…and to the excellent, in whom is all my delight." Excellency, according to Webster, is "meritoriously near the standard or model; very good of its kind; first-class state or possessing good qualities in an eminent degree; exalted merit." Who would not desire this for their children or charges? God's Word certainly has a great deal to say about the subject that ought to inspire those of us who have the responsibility of rearing children for the Lord or of training and teaching young people. Read carefully these verses, paying special attention to the words in bold:

II Timothy 2:15   *Study to shew thyself **approved** unto God, a **workman** that needeth not to be ashamed…*

Philippians 1:10a   *That ye may approve things that are **excellent**…*

Ecclesiastes 2:13	*Then I saw that **wisdom excelleth folly**...*
James 4:17	*Therefore to him that **knoweth to do good**, and doeth it not, to him it is sin.*
I Corinthians 10:31	*...whatsoever ye do, do **all** to the glory of God.*
Ecclesiastes 9:10	***Whatsoever** thy hand findeth to do, do it with thy **might**...*

These are the attitudes and responses that a Christ-honoring servant of God will desire to have in his life and to inculcate in the lives of others. So much of this is determined by two factors: first is the leadership. Is it truly our desire to see those we train do an excellent job and to do all they can to have their lives count for the Savior? Remember, as Dr. Lee Roberson has so long stated, "Everything rises and falls on leadership." Secondly, what is the attitude of the listener? Have we shown the student that God is only truly pleased when we do our absolute best for Him? We must stress that our ability to ultimately succeed in the spectrum of eternity rests totally in the hands of God. "I can do all things through Christ which strengtheneth me." (Philippians 4:13) We must help them to understand the value of a single life dedicated to the service of the Almighty.

Unfortunately, many young people do not view their lives as being a matter of importance. This perception of value is extremely important and can color both choices and actions throughout the course of an entire life span.

Years ago, a young man was making his way down a street in the immediate proximity of a large construction site. With the unbridled curiosity and enthusiasm of youth, he questioned each worker he passed with the phrase, "What are you doing?" Worker number one answered with a snarl and said, "I'm laying bricks." Worker number two said, "Son, I'm working so I can feed my family." Worker number three said, "Young man, I'm trying to help build the most beautiful cathedral this city has ever seen." Undoubtedly, most readers would be prone to suspect that the last worker was doing the best job. It is our job to inspire vision as to what others can do for the cause of the Lord. We truly are our brother's keeper, but we are also his mentor and model. Think of the value of a mother like Susannah Wesley, who patiently spent her waking hours loving and teaching her children. As one visits her grave in Bunhill field on the outskirts of London, it becomes readily apparent that those hands that rocked the cradle of John and Charles Wesley over two hundred years ago truly affected the world. Who is it that God has for us to train and develop? Of course, we must start with our own children, but then there undoubtedly will be those – a youth group, a Sunday school class, a ball team, or various other opportunities – that God will have made available to us.

Areas of Responsibility

So many of these topics will seem to some to be obvious or even commonly accepted, but with each ensuing year we see less evidence of responsibility in areas such as these. This can only be traced to the fact that emphasis has lagged or disappeared. Those of us in a position of training must remember that where we sow an emphasis, we will reap a harvest.

1) ***Manners*** – It is almost quaint to hear young people today say, "Yes, Sir," or "Yes, Ma'am." *Please* has become a word almost delegated to the dustbin of the serious scrabble players, and no more honor is given to the senior saints of the church than to the mannequin in the department store window. Brethren, these things ought not so to be...(James 3:10)

Honor toward adults, toward those older than us, and toward items as different as the Bible and the national anthem ought to be reestablished. The day when young people stood when an adult entered the room or patiently stood and saluted during the national anthem does not have to be ancient history. While actions like these are obviously not natural, we are immediately reminded that we must crucify the flesh daily. Of course, no one says that it will be easy to revive the manners that were commonplace in Victorian society, but it is still something that needs to receive a new emphasis.

Other areas of manners should also be instilled while charges are young. Whether it is proper behavior in God's house, or proper etiquette at a restaurant or another public place, there is definitely a need for a revival of responsibility in this entire realm. Regarding how to do so, praise for good and a punishment for bad still apply.

2) ***Thinking*** – IBM used to be famous for its one word credo plastered throughout its computing empire. The credo simply said, *THINK.* The age-old refrain, "I just didn't think about it" seems to be in vogue now more than ever. But thinking processes and subject material are both of highest importance because God's Word says, "For as he thinketh in his heart, so is he:" (Proverbs 23:7) It is crucial to help young people to know how to think and what to think about. This is why, as parents, we need to be so careful as to what is going in the ear and eye gates. Much of

today's thinking processes have been formed through watching the convoluted and humanistic principles played out on television and video. Combined with the misogynistic message in the world's music, we can certainly see why it is harder for this generation to truly live a holy life than any in recent memory. The 1960's television of *Flipper*, *Ozzie and Harriet*, *My Three Sons*, and *I Love Lucy* is no more. Screen classics like *Ben Hur* or *Swiss Family Robinson* would not find many watchers today. Even the old *Hardy Boys* and *Nancy Drew* series have been replaced by fare that panders to the flesh. A word to the wise parent or teacher: Be watchful as to the reading material in your home. The horror novels of a Stephen King or V.C. Andrews are a far cry from the "scary stories" told around campfires of yesteryear.

While it is crucial to be cognizant of what young people are thinking about, it is also imperative to help them to learn to think. There are three broad avenues that can lead to improvement in this area. They are listening skills, ability to follow directions, and problem solving. One cannot overemphasize the importance of each of these. Truly these skills could be combined into the single heading of decision-making. This is an area that desperately needs the attention of those in authority. To allow this to be self-taught is to ask for tragedy. Practice, drill, and repetition are all effective at bringing these traits into regular practice.

3) *Work* – Why do we now marvel at young people whom we say are "hard workers?" Paul told the Corinthian church that we are "labourers together with God." (I Corinthians 3:9) Songwriter Isaac Watts understood it well when he said we are not "to be carried through the skies on flowery beds of ease while others toil to win the prize and sail through bloody seas." We have a work to do. The ministry is work, and to truly minister is work.

164

Therefore, if we are serious about those we work with truly accomplishing something with their lives, they must learn that it will entail work. What a tremendous promise to know that our "labour is not in vain in the Lord." (I Corinthians 15:58) That which is done for Christ truly will last. The extra mile is not just the creation of some positive mental attitude guru. No, God's Word says that if your brother asks you "to go a mile, go with him twain." (Matthew 5:41) In Matthew 5:46-48, the Lord Jesus sets some high standards for His followers when He made it clear that He expects more from us than from publicans who were living for their works. The rhetorical question in Matthew 5:47 ought to ring loudly in our ears today. *What are we doing more than others?*

God's attitude toward the sluggard and toward slothfulness in general is well delineated throughout the book of Proverbs. Unfortunately, it seems as if our Christian homes are allowing the mentality of our socialistic welfare state to permeate our homes and our schools. Work still needs to be assigned to our young charges. And while it is true that children are a blessing from the Lord, children themselves do not need to act as if their parents are the "lucky chosen" because of their presence. It is time that young people begin again to work so they can once again appreciate how blessed they really are. Maybe if students had to pay for half of summer or winter camp, or two thirds of all extra clothes beyond that which would be a necessity, attitudes would change. With almost a quarter-century of college experience, I highly recommend that parents require their children to pay for half of their school bill. It has astounded administrators for years how that many who have their way totally paid for can produce some of the worst grades. It is clear to many that without cost and ownership, there is often no need seen for great effort. Other areas that could certainly receive like attention would be car payments and car insurance. Paying half of additional premiums with explanations of the inflationary effect of accidents or tickets should certainly have a positive effect on the adolescent drivers of our country.

Of course, all of these ultimately reflect back on the work ethic. During Biblical times, the patriarchs disdained that which would cost them nothing. (Genesis 23:13-16; II Samuel 24:21-24) Certainly the pendulum has swung far from those philosophical moorings during the intervening millennia. Couples with young children will often ask for abbreviated advice regarding child rearing. Unfailingly I will say to teach a work ethic, obedience, and respect for authority.

4) *Obedience* – "...to obey is better than sacrifice, and to hearken than the fat of rams." (I Samuel 15:22) "Children, obey your parents in the Lord: for this is right. Honor thy father and mother... That it may be well with thee, and thou mayest live long on the earth." (Ephesians 6:1-3) "Obey them that have the rule over you, and submit yourselves: for they watch for your souls, as they that must give an account..." (Hebrews 13:17) God's law for the family found in Ephesians 5-6 is clearly for husbands to love, wives to submit, and children to obey. God's Word teaches that the father is the spiritual head of the home, the high priest of the family. As a child learns to submit to and to obey his parents in childhood, he is also learning proper response to God in adulthood.

The best way to eradicate disobedience is to let the child know that there is always an earned consequence for failing to obey. The consequence of the laxness in our country's legal system toward some multiple offenders has led habitual criminals to believe that crime can pay. Such was certainly not the case in Old Testament times when an eye for an eye was exacted. Even in colonial days, miscreants who flaunted the laws of society realized that if they

166

were caught, there would be dire consequences. Suffice it to say, groups like the ACLU, People for the American Way, and Amnesty International have brought about great changes in how justice is both perceived and dispensed.

If this principle of obedience can be engrained into our children's and students' lives, it will undoubtedly make life easier and better for both the child and parent alike. Don't back down, don't equivocate, don't waffle – stand by your word and demand obedience. This is something that God wants, and so should we.

5) *To Seek God's Will and Way* – Statements concerning God's will can encompass such wide boundaries that we often are afraid to enter its boundaries. Certainly we would include our ultimate service for the Lord, but during training times, issues such as an attitude of submission (opposite of pride), a forgiving spirit, and a personal, ecclesiastical, and general dedication are all areas that need to be taught. Salvation, while the single most important decision one can make, is but the first in a list of important choices.

Examples of Responsibility

It is a poor teacher or parent who says, "Do as I say and not as I do." More than ever before, the Christian young people need godly examples. Despite his astounding athletic ability, Michael Jordan with his gambling, drinking, smoking, and marital difficulties makes an extremely poor role model for the Christian young person. Certainly Jordan has worked very hard to become the best in the field of basketball, but I do not want him to be my son's hero.

Obviously the adults that are closest to a young person have the greatest opportunity to influence him via their example. This ought to be a sobering challenge to parents, teachers, and youth workers alike.

God's Word gives the Christian a multitude of exemplary characters whose lives are worthy examples. Above all, we must point people to the Lord Jesus Christ. We are to strive to be like the One who came "to minister and to give His life a ransom for many." Once we have pointed young people to the supreme Example, we ought to point out the many stellar lives from which the Holy Spirit saw fit to allow us to learn. Joseph and Daniel, Moses and Joshua, Paul and Peter begin a list of illustrious characters from which we can garner so much. Ruth and Esther are sterling examples for young ladies of today. Others, like Simeon and Anna, whose names are not as well known, are certainly worthy of our attention. The library of the Bible's sixty-six books contains enough examples if that were all that were available. But others stand tall through the pages of church and secular history alike.

It is our duty to share with the young the examples of those who have preceded them. In my own life, my father's constancy in Bible study, memorization, review of verses, and commitment to personal soul winning will remain with me as long as I retain lucid thinking processes. Many young people have not grown up with this type of home background and need an example to show them the way.

It is extremely important, especially with those who are younger, to take the time to draw out applications. An illustration would be to show how that prior to David being a sovereign, he was first a son, a shepherd, a soldier, and a servant. Or show how Joseph and Daniel remained true to principles even when far from home and ostensibly out of sight of authority. Or Elisha, who stayed close to God's man, worked hard, had a high regard for his family, and was willing to be a follower and a servant. (I Kings 19:19-21)

From an entirely different perspective, we can see people who believed in a dream and sacrificed every thing till that dream became a reality. Whether a Ford or a Wright, a Lindbergh or an Edison, the examples are many. We as mentors must make the testimonies of these men come alive in the hearts and minds of our charges, inspiring them to believe that they, too, can make a difference in this world - for Christ.

Practical Responsibilities

If we are to see a true revival of responsibility, we will have to do more than model responsible behavior. The more areas in which a young person can begin practicing responsible behavior, the more this will become ingrained into his persona. The chart below gives a few ideas of habits that can be encouraged, divided by age group:

Pre-school   *Pick up toys personally, straighten shoes, clean things off the floor in personal area.*

Elementary   *Bible reading time, neat room, clothes in place, homework or music practice done correctly (extra praise if the child attempts to work before play), brushing teeth and combing or brushing hair, jobs around the house like taking small trash cans out to be emptied into a larger trash can, Bible memory work regarding reading assignments, helping clear the table, light housekeeping.*

Jr./Sr. High   *Music lessons, homework, jobs and regular responsibilities around the home, dishes, cooking and sewing assignments for young ladies, typing practice for both boys and girls, learning or some trade for young men in an apprenticeship-type program, washing the family vehicles, yard work, vacuuming, window washing.*

It will quickly be seen that very few of these will be maintained with a total volunteer spirit. Practice and praise will combine to make these a starting point of responsibility in a young person's life.

It should be noted that since much of America has transitioned totally away from an agrarian setting, many of the daily chores that were just "part" of farm life have dissipated, if not entirely disappeared. This would include splitting wood, collecting eggs, and milking cows, as well as a number of other incidental but necessary chores that make up farm life. Some of these chores were considered especially rancorous, such as the seemingly interminable hoeing during summer. But tasks such as these did more than just build calluses; they also developed a work ethic.

The lack of many of these daily jobs begs for a replacement. Two effective tools are individual music instruction and team sports, especially when connected with a Christian school. Sports can teach a wide variety of lessons, including personal discipline, teamwork, and striving for a goal. It is also wise to keep teenagers busy and avoid the opportunity for mischief or outright sin in those after-school hours. Of course, the coach will become a major influence factor. As to music, the daily regimen of practice is invaluable in the teaching of responsibility. Of course, music can be used widely in the cause of Christ, and this should affect the choice of teacher as well as the curriculum studied by the student. It should be made clear to the student that the lessons are paid for sacrificially by the parents and that practice is a prerequisite for their continuation.

In the field of academia, teachers also have a tremendous responsibility to develop this area of life. Some of the tools that can be used to accomplish this would include homework, projects, reports, and, of course, tests and quizzes. It is important for the teacher to be mindful of church activities such as teen visitation or revival and to give these preeminence. This in itself will teach young people something about proper priorities. The other side of the coin is to have classes where academic responsibility is stressed and where teachers themselves are examples of principle through their obvious organization, ability to stay on track, and finishing the entire textbook. Memorization, although ridiculed by some, is still a necessary part of the educational process. Speech contests for all grades are a wonderful way to begin to get young people to pay the price to learn to memorize something as well as develop communication skills. After all, each student will in all probability be speaking every day for the rest of his life.

Living responsibly in life certainly is more difficult than living with a derelict, "Qué será, será" attitude. But there is the difference between following wherever the streams of life are flowing and the king salmon personality, who is willing to fight his way upstream, even jumping over obstacles to accomplish a goal. It is worth noting that few gamesmen show an interest in mounting a carp on the study wall. So we as molders and mentors will be far prouder someday of the ones who have principles coursing through them and are living a life marked by character, consistency, and above all, Christ-likeness.

Conclusion

"And the things that thou hast heard of me among many witnesses, the same commit thou to faithful men, who shall be able to teach others also." II Timothy 2:2

A black pastor of a Baptist church was speaking to a group of college students one day and said: "Children, you're going to die! . . . One of these days, they're going to take you out to the cemetery, drop you in a hole, throw some dirt on your face, and go back to the church and eat potato salad.

"When you were born, you alone were crying and everybody else was happy. The important question I want to ask is this: When you die are you alone going to be happy, leaving everyone else crying? The answer depends on whether you live to get titles or you live to get testimonies. When they lay you in the grave, are people going to stand around reciting the fancy titles you earned, or are they going to stand around giving testimonies of the good things you did for them? . . . Will you leave behind just some newspaper column telling people how important you were, or will you leave crying people who give testimonies of how they've lost the best friend they ever had?

There's nothing wrong with titles. Titles are good things to have. But if it ever comes down to a choice between a title or a testimony – go for the testimony."[1]

We live on after death in two ways. We live on in eternity forever with Christ, and we live on in the lives of those that we mentor. The Lord Jesus Christ poured His life into a few men and women during His three years of earthly ministry. He mentored ignorant fishermen and corrupt tax collectors and radicals into a powerful cohesive force which ultimately would change the world.

Jesus never ruled a nation, led an army, or wrote a book. Yet His message lives today in every corner of the world. It didn't happen because Jesus was a master of mass communication techniques, or management skills, or leadership training, but because He was a mentor. He invested His life and message in people.

Today, we get caught up in big numbers. We dream of preaching to the masses in large crusades, or via radio or television. The average pastor, teacher, or parent, however, will never stand before millions or thousands or maybe even hundreds of people at any given time. That is why there is such a desperate need for us to shift our attention in ministry to the mentoring process. II Timothy 2:2 commands us to take the message that we have received to someone else and then mentor them in such a way that they in turn will take it to another. If you were to reach one person with the Gospel in the next calendar year and mentor them in the Word of God, so that the following year, they along with you could reach one person and mentor them, and so on – do you know what the results would be? Well, by this time next year instead of just you, there would be two. Two years from now there

---

[1] Ron Lee Davis, *Mentoring: The Strategy of the Master*, Nashville, TN, Thomas Nelson Publishing, 1991, pp. 213-214.

would be four – the following year eight, and so on. Guess how many people your "one" life could impact in 35 years if you just mentored one a year and they in turn did likewise? If my math is right, in 35 years, following the formula of II Timothy 2:2, over 17 billion people would be reached – almost three times the present world population! I think it is safe to say that none of us will ever pastor a church of 17 billion, or teach 17 billion students in our career as a teacher – but by following the example of Christ, we can reach the world through the mentoring of one person at a time.

Blaise Pascal once said, "The present is never our goal: the past and the present are our means: the future alone is our goal."[2] What a joy it would be for us one day to look back on our ministry and realize that it didn't end with a sermon, or a lesson, or a few years in our homes, but it lives on in the lives of those that we influenced and continues to multiply through them.

The ultimate success of my life will not be judged by the number of those who admire me for my accomplishments, but by the number of those who attribute their wholeness to my love for them – by the number of those who have seen their true beauty and worth in my eyes.[3]

Boris Kornfeld was a Russian Jew imprisoned in one of Stalin's notorious gulags. Though trained as a doctor, Kornfeld's medical skills were largely wasted in a place where human life was a cheap and degraded commodity. Assigned a position in the prison hospital, most of the "medicine" he was allowed to practice involved the signing of false medical documents which allowed the guards to place prisoners in solitary torture chambers. The

---

[2] Kenneth O. Gangel and Warren S. Benson, *Christian Education: It's History and Philosophy*, Chicago, IL, Moody Press, 1983, p. 367.
[3] Davis, p. 211

documents stated that the prisoners were physically strong enough to endure the punishment; Kornfeld knew those men would die.

Kornfeld despised Christianity. He had grown up embracing communism and hating the Christian religion of the Czars, who had persecuted Russian Jews. Yet, though he had always been a committed communist, Kornfeld had been accused of some crime against the State and was now condemned to spend the rest of his life in prison. Now, disillusioned and betrayed by his atheistic "religion" called communism, Kornfeld was a man without hope or faith.

While in prison, he encountered a fellow prisoner who told him about a Jewish Messiah who had come many centuries before to fulfill the promises God made to Israel. The man told Kornfeld that this Jesus had come to the Jews first, and now called all of mankind to Himself. As the other prisoner recited the Lord's Prayer to him, Kornfeld found himself strangely moved and attracted to this Christian message he had previously rejected.

Eventually, Kornfeld's Christian friend was taken away to an unknown fate. Yet the Gospel message continued to creep slowly into Boris Kornfeld's heart. Over a period of months, Kornfeld began to feel changed and warmed. The hatred he felt toward the cruel guards and officers began to melt. His despair turned to hope.

Yet, his conscience troubled him. Kornfeld knew he could no longer sign the false documents and be a party to sending his fellow prisoners to their deaths. He knew he couldn't change the fate of the doomed men. But he also knew he could no longer endure that stain on his soul. So he refused to sign.

It was around this time that he caught an orderly stealing food from a dying man in the prison hospital. Before his conversion, Kornfeld would have turned a blind eye to the incident. Now, with a Christian sense of right and wrong, he knew he had to report the orderly's actions to the prison officials, even though the orderlies were known to take revenge against "stoolies." The orderly received three days in the punishment block, then was released.

A few days later, Kornfeld was in the hospital, checking on patients, when he came upon a man who had just had an operation for intestinal cancer. Even though the patient was groggy and incoherent from the anesthetic, Kornfeld began to talk to him. He told the patient about the change that had come over his heart after someone shared the Gospel with him. He shared about the forgiveness and hope he felt in his heart, despite the cruelty and misery of the gulag. Even in his anesthetic fog, the patient clung to Kornfeld's words until he finally fell asleep.

Hours later, when the patient awoke, the man in the next bed told him the news that was being whispered all over the hospital: Dr. Kornfeld was dead. During the night, someone had crushed his skull with a mallet while he lay sleeping.

The patient was stricken with grief. But he was also filled with the conviction that Jesus was now alive within himself, that the life and faith that had been inside of Boris Kornfeld had somehow been transferred into his own being. The doctor had died, but the patient had lived.

The patient's name was Alexander Solzhenitsyn. Kornfeld had performed the beautiful act of "heart to heart resuscitation," pouring the last remaining drops of his life into Solzhenitsyn. Kornfeld never knew the powerful effect his witness had, not only on Solzhenitsyn, but through him, upon the entire world. In the last hours of his life, Boris Kornfeld lived the life-style of a mentor.[4] May God allow you and me to live our lives as mentors!

---

[4] Ibid, pp. 201-203.

---◇---

"Through the process of mentoring, we have the privilege of writing the history of the future."

"It is better to fail in a cause that will ultimately succeed, than to succeed in a cause that will ultimately fail."   - Peter Marshall

Bibliography

Berg, Jim. *Changed into His Image.* Greenville, SC, Bob Jones University Press. 1999.

Blattner, John C., ed. *Leading Christians to Maturity*. Ann Arbor, MI, The Center for Pastoral Renewal. 1987.

Burns, Jim. *The Youth Builder*. Eugene, OR, Harvest House Publishers. 1988.

Clark, Robert, E., Lin Johnson, Allyn K. Sloat, ed. *Christian Education: Foundations for the Future*. Chicago, IL, Moody Press. 1991.

Davis, Ron Lee. *Mentoring: The Strategy of the Master*. Nashville, TN, Thomas Nelson Publishers. 1991.

Downs, Perry G. *Teaching for Spiritual Growth*. Grand Rapids, MI, Zondervan Publishing House. 1994.

Eavey, C. B. *History of Christian Education*. Chicago, IL, Moody Press. 1964.

Eims, Leroy. *Be The Leader You Were Meant To Be*. Wheaton, IL, Victor Books. 1976.

Flattery, George M. *Teaching for Christian Maturity*. Springfield, MO, Gospel Publishing House. 1968.

Gangel, Kenneth O., Warren S. Benson. *Christian Education: Its History and Philosophy*. Chicago, IL, Moody Press. 1983.

Gregory, John Milton. *The Seven Laws of Teaching*. Revised Edition. Grand Rapids, MI, Baker Book House. 1954.

Habecker, Eugéne B. *The Other Side of Leadership*, Wheaton, IL, Victor Books. 1987.

Heidebrecht, Paul, Jerry Rohrbach. *Fathering a Son*. Chicago, IL, Moody Press. 1979.

Henderson, T. S. *The Good Teacher*. Philadelphia, PA, American Baptist Publishing Society. [No date printed].

Hendricks, Howard G. *Teaching to Change Lives*. Portland, OR, Multnomah Press. 1987.

Horton, Ronald A. ed. *Christian Education: Its Mandate and Mission*. Greenville, SC, Bob Jones University Press. 1992.

Richards, Lawrence O. *Christian Education*. Grand Rapids, MI, Zondervan Publishing House. 1975.

Stormer, John A. *None Dare Call It Education*. Florissant, MO, Liberty Bell Press. 1998.

Swindoll, Charles R. ed. *The Tale of the Tardy Oxcart*. Nashville, TN, Word Publishing. 1998.

Tripp, Tedd. *Shepherding a Child's Heart*. Wapwallopen, PA, Shepherd Press. 1995.

Wilkinson, Bruce. *The Seven Laws of the Learner*. Textbook Edition. Sisters, OR, Multnomah Press. 1992.